COWBOY SONGS FOR UKULELE

ISBN 978-1-4803-3998-9

HAL•LEONARD®
CORPORATION

7777 W. BLUEMOUND RD. P.O. BOX 13819 MILWAUKEE, WI 53213

Visit Hal Leonard Online at
www.halleonard.com

CONTENTS

Abilene

Words and Music by Lester Brown, John D. Loudermilk and Bob Gibson

Along the Navajo Trail

Words and Music by Dick Charles, Larry Markes and Eddie De Lange

Back in the Saddle Again

Words and Music by Gene Autry and Ray Whitley

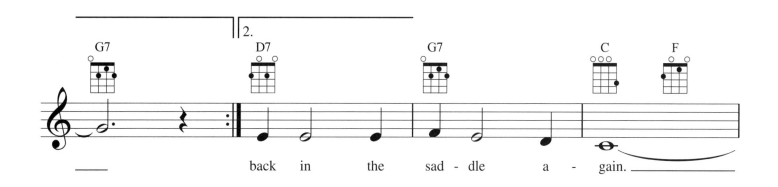

back in the sad - dle a - gain. _____

Chorus

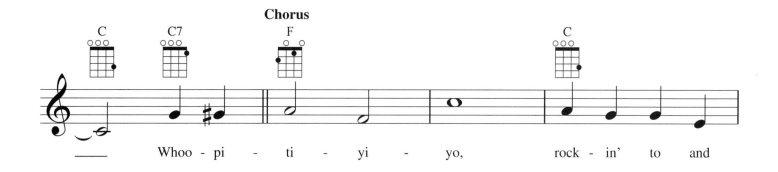

_____ Whoo - pi - ti - yi - yo, rock - in' to and

fro, back in the sad - dle a - gain. _____

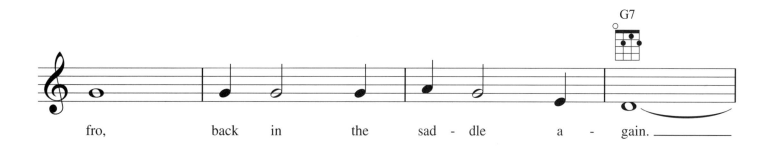

_____ Whoo - pi - ti - yi - yay, I go my way, __

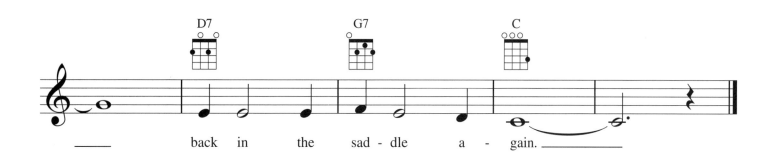

_____ back in the sad - dle a - gain. _____

Billy Barlow

Collected, Adapted and Arranged by John A. Lomax and Alan Lomax

1. Let's go hunt-ing, says Risk - y Rob. Let's go
2.–7. *See additional lyrics*

hunt - ing, says Rob - in to Bob. Let's go hunt - ing, says Dan - iel to

Joe. Let's go hunt - ing, says Bil - ly Bar - low.

Additional Lyrics

2. What shall I hunt? says Risky Rob.
What shall I hunt? says Robin to Bob.
What shall I hunt? says Daniel to Joe.
Hunt for a rat, says Billy Barlow.

3. How shall I get him? says Risky Rob.
How shall I get him? says Robin to Bob.
How shall I get him? says Daniel to Joe.
Borrow a gun, says Billy Barlow.

4. How shall we divide him? says Risky Rob.
How shall we divide him? says Robin to Bob.
How shall we divide him? says Daniel to Joe.
Hack him to pieces, says Billy Barlow.

5. I'll take a shoulder, says Risky Rob.
I'll take a side, says Robin to Bob.
I'll take a ham, says Daniel to Joe.
Tail bone mine, says Billy Barlow.

6. How shall we cook him? says Risky Rob.
How shall we cook him? says Robin to Bob.
How shall we cook him? says Daniel to Joe.
Each as you like it, says Billy Barlow.

7. I'll broil shoulder, says Risky Rob.
I'll fry side, says Robin to Bob.
I'll boil ham, says Daniel to Joe.
Tail bone raw, says Billy Barlow.

Buffalo Gals
(Won't You Come Out Tonight?)

Words and Music by Cool White (John Hodges)

Bury Me Not on the Lone Prairie

Words based on the poem "The Ocean Burial" by Rev. Edwin H. Chapin
Music by Ossian N. Dodge

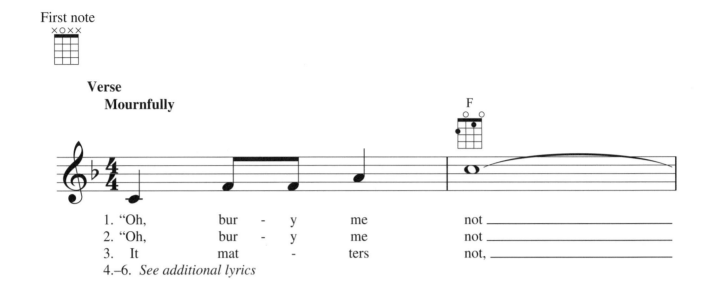

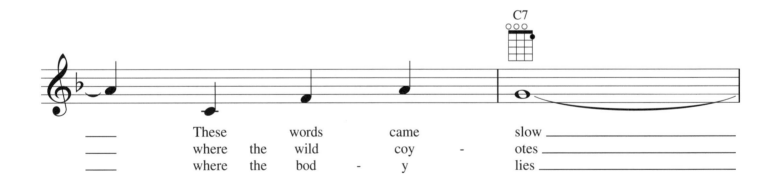

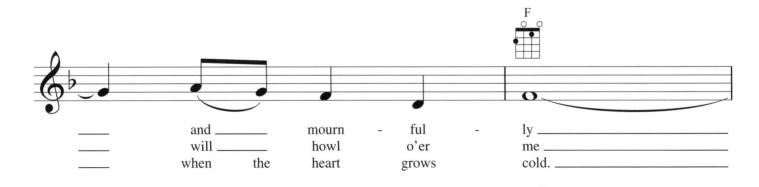

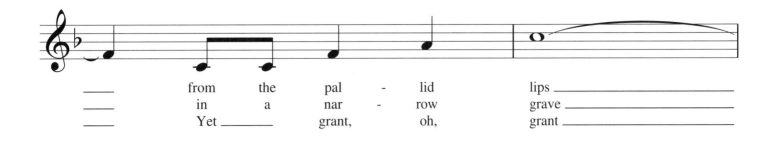

from the pal - lid lips _____
in a nar - row grave _____
Yet _____ grant, oh, grant _____

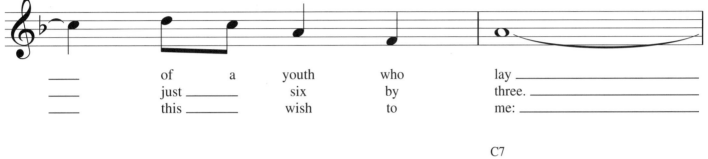

of a youth who lay _____
just _____ six by three. _____
this _____ wish to me: _____

C7

on his dy - ing bed _____
Oh, _____ bur - y me not _____
Oh, _____ bur - y me not _____

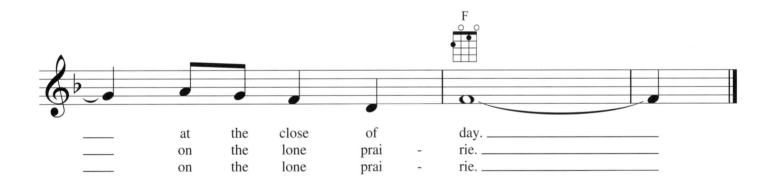

F

at the close of day. _____
on the lone prai - rie. _____
on the lone prai - rie. _____

Additional Lyrics

4. I've always wished to be laid when I died
   In the little churchyard on the green hillside.
   By my father's grave there let mine be,
   And bury me not on the lone prairie."

5. "Oh, bury me not," and his voice failed there,
   But we took no heed of his dying prayer.
   In a narrow grave just six by three,
   We buried him there on the lone prairie.

6. And the cowboys now as they roam the plain,
   For they marked the spot where his bones were lain,
   Fling a handful of roses o'er his grave,
   With a prayer to Him who his soul will save.

Call of the Canyon

Words and Music by Billy Hill

Columbus Stockade Blues

Words and Music by Jimmie Davis and Eva Sargent

friends   all   turned   their   backs   on   me.
I   was   peep - ing   through   the   bars.
bro - ken   up   our   hap - py   home.

Well, you can

Chorus

go   and   leave   me   if   you   want   to.

Nev - er   let   it   cross   your   mind,

for   in   your   heart _____ you   love   an - oth -

1., 2.

er.   Leave,   lit - tle   dar - lin';   I   don't   mind. _____

3.

_____   2. Last _____   mind. _____
3. Man - y

The Cowboy Blues

Words and Music by Cindy Walker

Cowboy's Heaven

Words and Music by Gene Autry and Frankie Marvin

First note

Verse

Moderately

G   C   A#°7

1. To - night I'm a tired, wea - ry cow - boy. _____ I've

(2.–4.) *See additional lyrics*

G   D7   G

been in the sad - dle all day, _____ search - ing the

C   G

hills and the val - leys _____ for cat - tle that

D7   G   D7

strayed a - way. _____ Old Paint is

G

tired and leg wea - ry. _____ His feet are

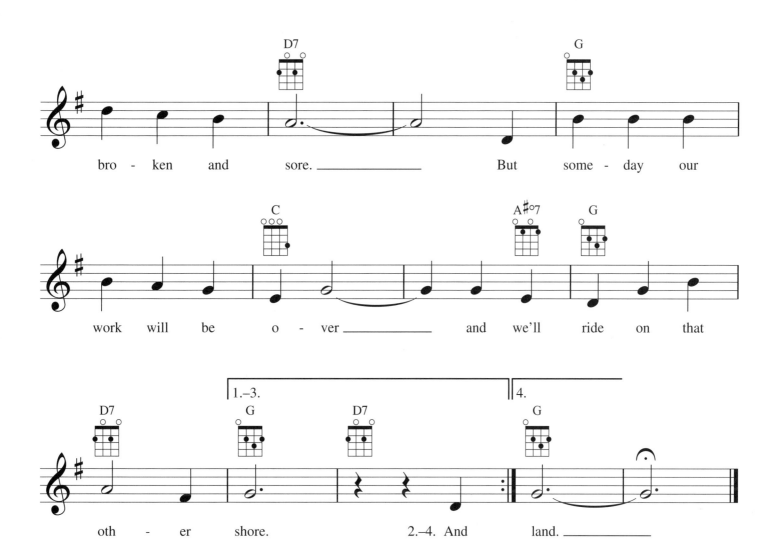

bro - ken and sore. _____ But some - day our

work will be o - ver _____ and we'll ride on that

oth - er shore. 2.–4. And land. _____

Additional Lyrics

2. And laying wrapped up in my blanket,
   Looking straight up in the sky,
   Watching the bright stars a-twinkling
   Away up there on high.
   Seems sometimes maybe they see us
   And maybe they understand.
   They may be the souls of cowpunchers
   And we'll come to that promised land.

3. And when I get way up there yonder,
   I will whistle softly and low,
   And my Old Paint horse will come running
   From some passing cloud pasture I know.
   I'll give him a handful of sugar
   And watch him say thanks with his eyes.
   I'll mount and then we'll be ready
   To report to the range boss on high.

4. And there'll be work up there a-plenty
   For a good cowpuncher someday,
   Keeping stray shootin' stars in the pasture,
   Riding herd on the Milky Way.
   The comets, they all must be mav'rick.
   They'll have to be marked with His brand.
   You bet me and Old Paint will be happy
   On that range on the promised land.

Dear Old Western Skies

Words and Music by Gene Autry

cat - tle ____ roam. _____ Dear old ____ west - ern ____

skies, there'll nev - er be ____ an - oth - er place that I call

Bridge

home. _____ Seems that I can hear the cat - tle low - -

ing, seems that I can see the pur - ple sage

Outro

blow - ing. I hope Old Paint and I will herd the do - gies by and

by un - der dear old west - ern skies. _____

Don't Take Your Guns to Town

Words and Music by Johnny R. Cash

First note

Verse
Moderately, in 2

1. A young cow-boy named Bil - ly Joe grew
(2.–5.) *See additional lyrics*

rest - less on the farm. A boy filled with

wan - der - lust, who real - ly meant no harm. He

changed his clothes and shined his boots and combed his dark hair

down, and his moth - er cried as he walked out: "Don't

Chorus

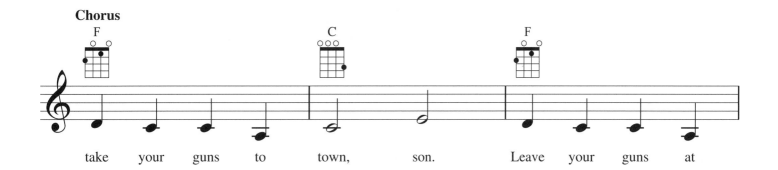

take your guns to town, son. Leave your guns at

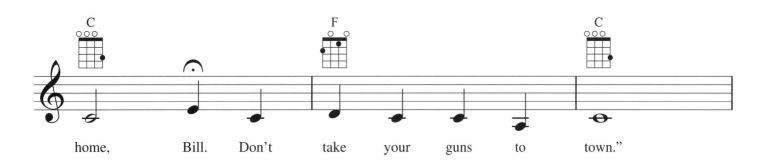

home, Bill. Don't take your guns to town."

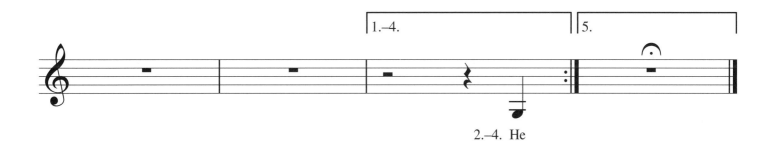

2.–4. He

Additional Lyrics

2. He laughed and kissed his mom and said, "Your Billy Joe's a man.
   I can shoot as quick and straight as anybody can.
   But I wouldn't shoot without a cause; I'd gun nobody down."
   But she cried again as he rode away:

3. He sang a song as on he rode, his guns hung at his hips.
   He rode into a cattle town, a smile upon his lips.
   He stopped and walked into a bar and laid his money down.
   But his mother's words echoed again:

4. He drank his first strong liquor then to calm his shaking hand,
   And tried to tell himself at last he had become a man.
   A dusty cowpoke at his side began to laugh him down,
   And he heard again his mother's words:

5. Filled with rage, then Billy Joe reached for his gun to draw.
   But the stranger drew his gun and fired it before he even saw.
   As Billy Joe fell to the floor the crowd all gathered 'round,
   And wondered at his final words:

Dude Ranch Cowhands

Words and Music by Gene Autry, Fred Rose and Johnny Marvin

First note

Verse

Lively, in 2

1. The Dude Ranch cow - hands don't do no work at
(2.–6.) See additional lyrics

all, be - cause they have no do - gies to round up in the

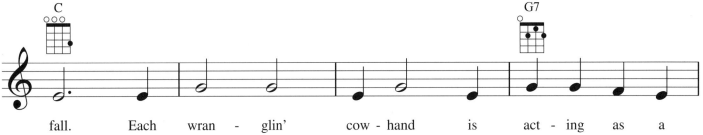

fall. Each wran - glin' cow - hand is act - ing as a

guide. He's round - in' up the moon - beams for the la - dy at his

Chorus

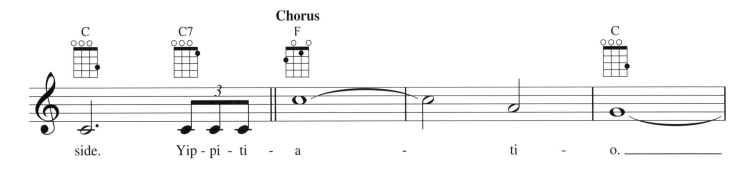

side. Yip - pi - ti - a - ti - o. _____

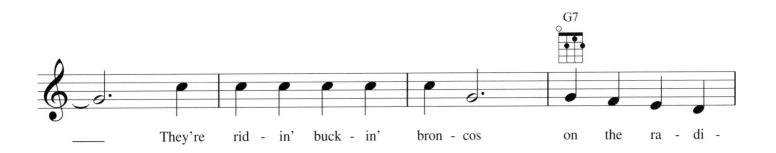

They're rid - in' buck - in' bron - cos on the ra - di -

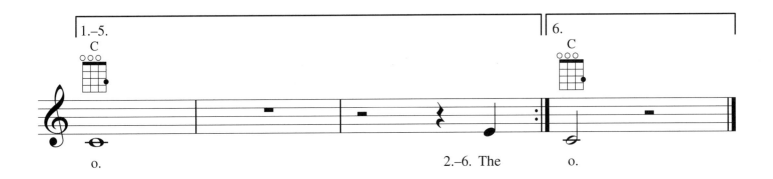

o. 2.–6. The o.

Additional Lyrics

2. The Dude Ranch cowhands are paler than the moon.
   They're always up till midnight and always sleep till noon.
   Those wranglin' cowhands demand the choicest roast.
   They once ate beans and bacon, but now it's quail on toast.

3. The Dude Ranch cowhands just work beneath the stars.
   Instead of brandin' cattle, they're strummin' on guitars.
   Each wranglin' cowhand has learned to harmonize
   With Kitty from the city while she gets her exercise.

4. The Dude Ranch cowhands play tennis, golf and bridge
   Instead of chasin' rustlers out across the ridge.
   Those wranglin' cowhands that never had a care
   Get wilder than a bronco if you even muss their hair.

5. The Dude Ranch cowhands can tell a dandy yarn,
   But when it comes to shootin' they couldn't hit a barn.
   Each wranglin' cowhand thinks he's a ridin' fool,
   But he learned his fancy ridin' in a correspondence school.

6. The Dude Ranch cowhands are burnin' up the plains.
   They're bouncin' in their saddles and oh! those aches and pains.
   Those wranglin' cowhands know every prairie call,
   But they'll all go back to Brooklyn when the work's all done this fall.

Dust

Words and Music by Gene Autry and Johnny Marvin

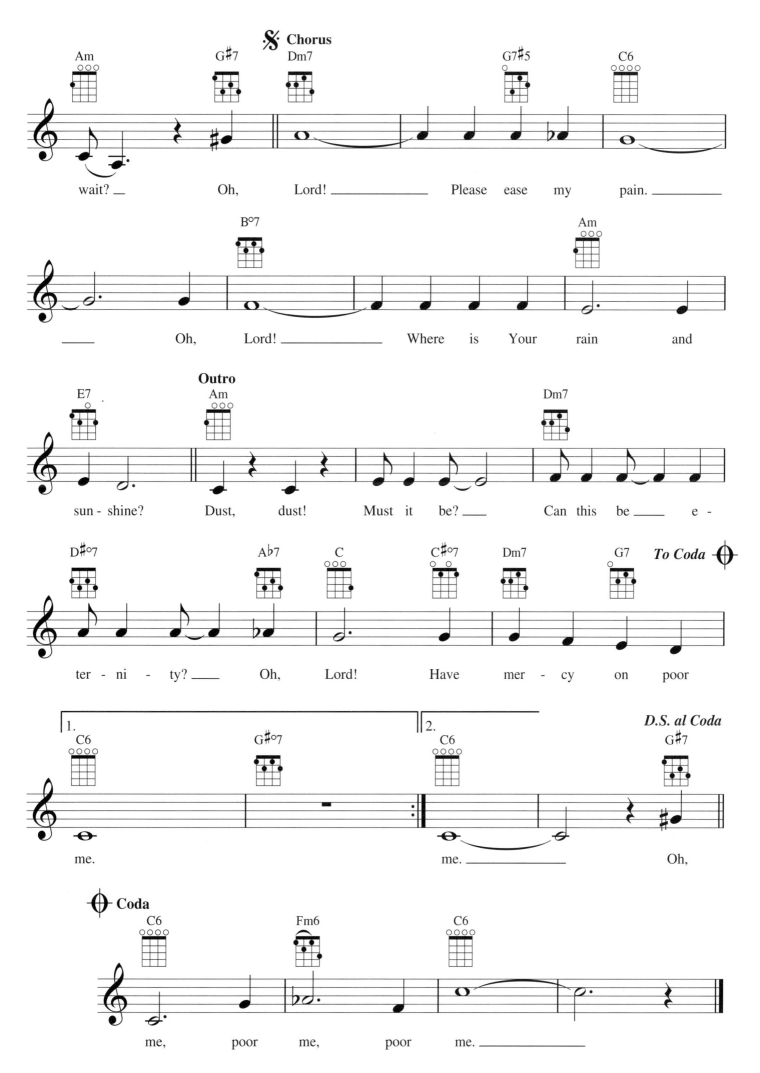

Empty Saddles

from RHYTHM ON THE RANGE
By Billy Hill

First note

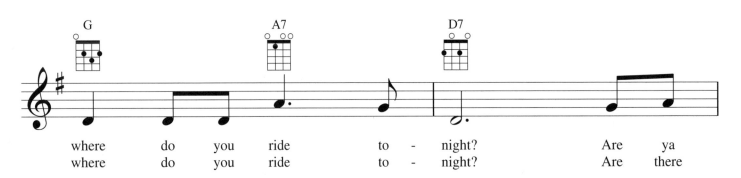

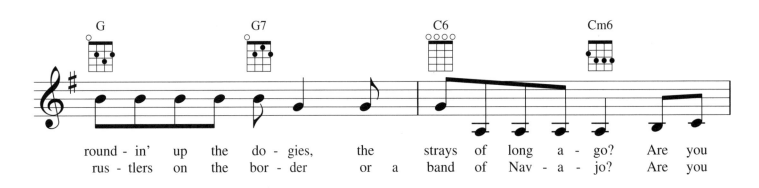

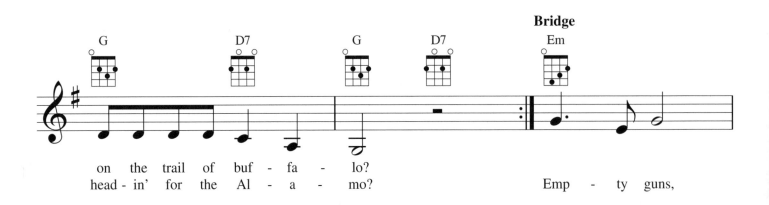

cov - ered with rust,   where   do you talk   to - night?

Emp - ty boots,   cov - ered with   dust,   where   do you walk   to -

Outro-Verse

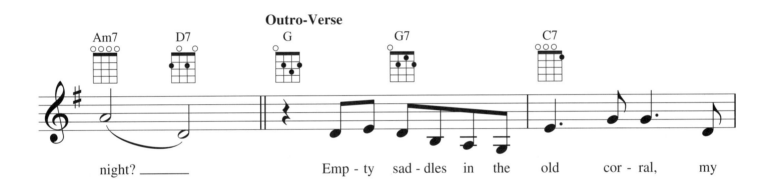

night? _____   Emp - ty sad - dles in the   old   cor - ral,   my

tears would be dried   to - night   if you'll on - ly say I'm lone - ly as you

car - ry my old pal, emp - ty   sad - dles in the old cor - ral.

(Ghost) Riders in the Sky

(A Cowboy Legend)

from RIDERS IN THE SKY
By Stan Jones

1. An old cow-poke went rid-ing out one dark and wind-y day.

(2.–4.) See additional lyrics

Up - on a ridge he rest - ed as he went a - long his way,

when all at once a might-y herd of red - eyed cows he saw a -

plow - in' thru the rag - ged skies and up the cloud - y draw.

Yi - pi - yi - ay, yi - pi - yi - o,

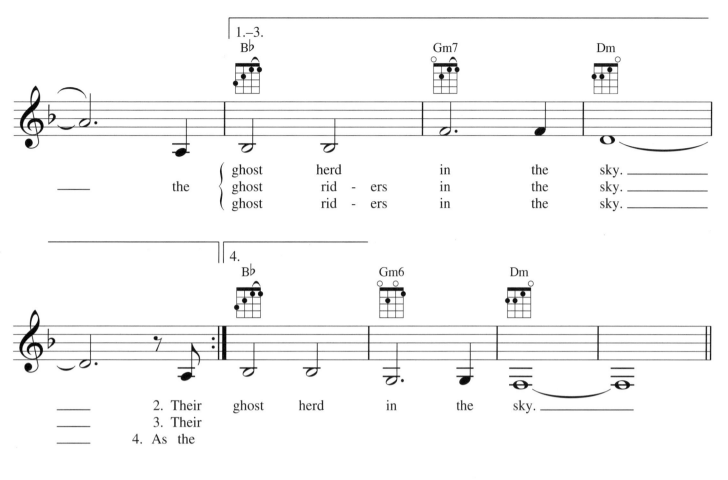

1.–3.
Bb   Gm7   Dm

the { ghost herd   in   the   sky. _____
      ghost rid - ers   in   the   sky. _____
      ghost rid - ers   in   the   sky. _____

4.
Bb   Gm6   Dm

_____ 2. Their   ghost   herd   in   the   sky. _____
_____ 3. Their
_____ 4. As the

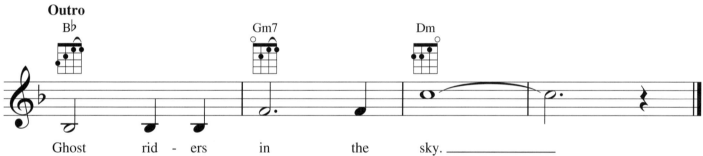

Outro
Bb   Gm7   Dm

Ghost rid - ers   in   the   sky. _____

Additional Lyrics

2. Their brands were still on fire and their hooves was made of steel.
   Their horns was black and shiny and their hot breath he could feel.
   A bolt of fear went through him as they thundered through the sky,
   For he saw the riders comin' hard as he heard their mournful cry.

3. Their faces gaunt, their eyes were blurred and shirts all soaked with sweat.
   They're ridin' hard to catch that herd, but they ain't caught them yet,
   'Cause they've got to ride forever on that range up in the sky
   On horses snortin' fire; as they ride on, hear their cry.

4. As the riders loped on by him, he heard one call his name.
   "If you want to save your soul from hell a-ridin' on our range,
   Then, cowboy, change your ways today or with us you will ride,
   A-tryin' to catch the devil's herd across these endless skies."

Happy Trails

from the Television Series THE ROY ROGERS SHOW
Words and Music by Dale Evans

First note

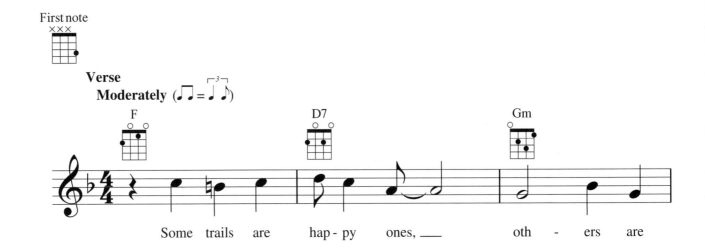

Some trails are hap-py ones, ___ oth - ers are

blue. It's the way you ride the trail that counts; ___ here's a

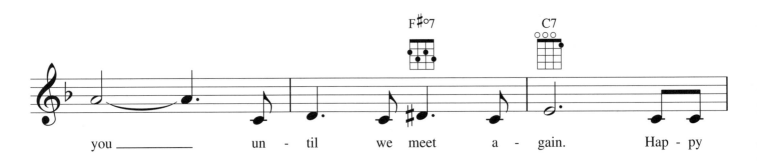

hap - py one for you. Hap - py trails to

you ___ un - til we meet a - gain. Hap - py

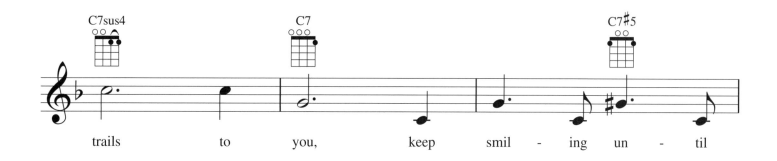

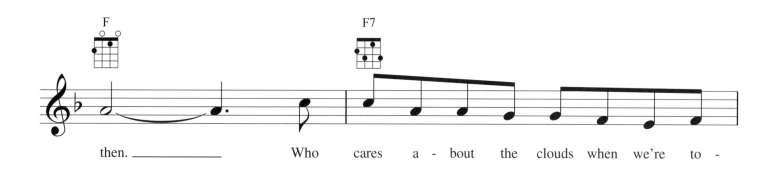

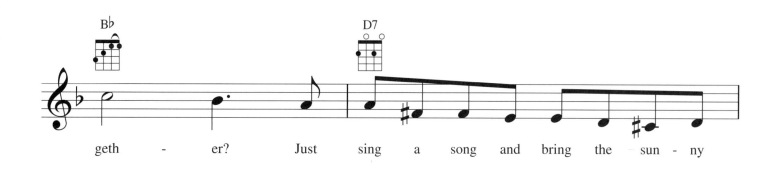

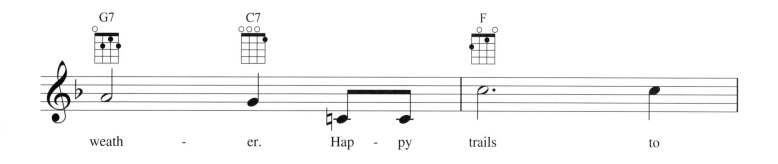

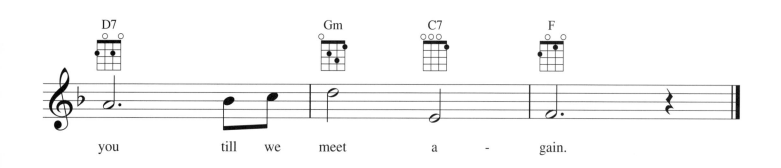

High Noon
(Do Not Forsake Me)

from HIGH NOON

Words by Ned Washington
Music by Dimitri Tiomkin

First note

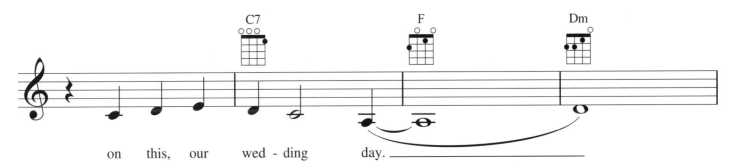

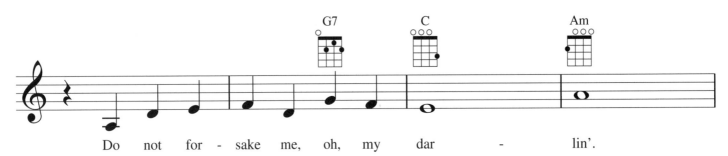

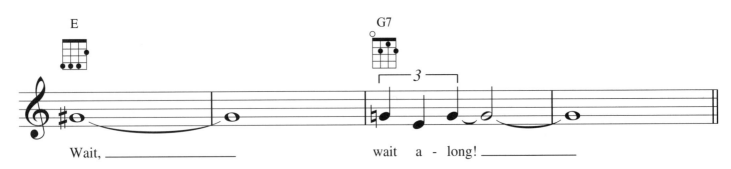

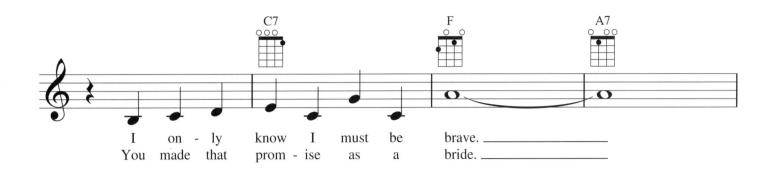

I on-ly know I must be brave. _____
You made that prom-ise as a bride. _____

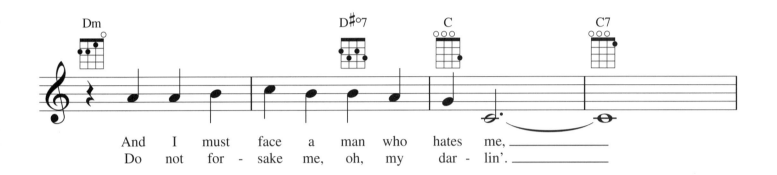

And I must face a man who hates me, _____
Do not for-sake me, oh, my dar-lin'. _____

or lie a cow-ard, a cra-ven cow-ard,
Al-though you're griev-in', don't think of leav-in',

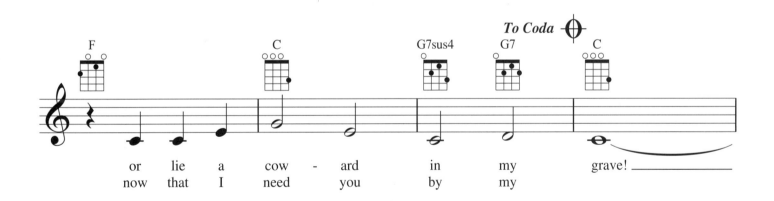

or lie a cow-ard in my grave! _____
now that I need you by my

Bridge

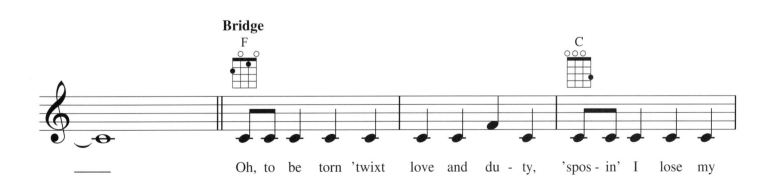

_____ Oh, to be torn 'twixt love and du-ty, 'spos-in' I lose my

fair - haired beau - ty. Look at the big hand move a - long ___ near - in' high noon.

He made a vow while in state's pris - on, vowed it would be my life or his - 'n.

I'm not a - fraid of death, but oh, ___ what will I

D.S. al Coda

do if you leave me?

Coda

side! ___ Wait a -

Outro

long, ___ wait a - long, ___ wait a -

long, ___ wait a - long! ___

The Colorado Trail

Traditional Cowboy Song

Hold On Little Dogies, Hold On

Words and Music by Gene Autry and Smiley Burnette

First note

Verse
Moderately

1. Col - ors are fly - in', to - day's the big show. The
(2.) ranch in Mon - tan - a we build a small fire. We
(3.) weav - in' through cac - tus I sing all day long, and the

cow - boys are whoop - in' the big ro - de - o. An -
rope and we brand in a way you'd ad - mire. With
hoot owls sing with me my cow - punch - er songs. I

nounc - ers are bus - y, the horns give a toot.
lar - i - at spin - ning and horse on the run, in
spy the stray do - gie go - ing o - ver the dune, and I

Cow - boys drive do - gies to the end of the chute.
twen - ty - one sec - onds the ___ hog - tie - in's done.
lust - i - ly sing him this ___ cow - punch - er tune.

Home on the Range

Lyrics by Dr. Brewster Higley
Music by Dan Kelly

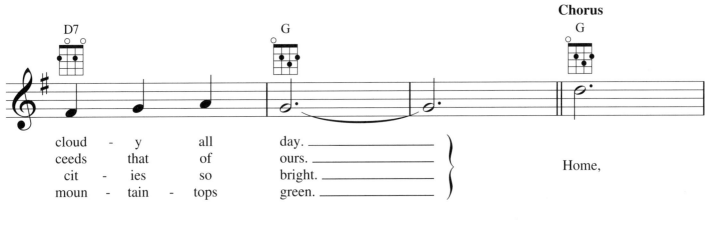

cloud - y all day. _____
ceeds that of ours. _____
cit - ies so bright. _____
moun - tain - tops green. _____

Home,

home on the range, _____ where the deer and the

an - te - lope play. _____ Where sel - dom is

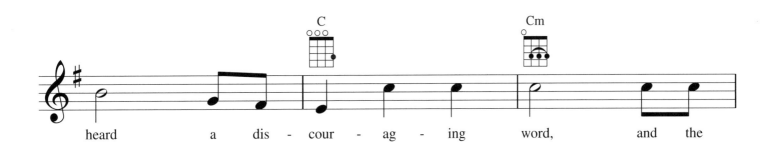

heard a dis - cour - ag - ing word, and the

skies are not cloud - y all day. _____

I Hate to Say Goodbye to the Prairie

Words and Music by Gene Autry and Odie Thompson

true. _____ I'll miss their cheer - y, "How - dy do, old pard -

ner." I'll miss the hap - py times I knew. _____

When the pur - ple sage blooms in the spring - time,

I'll be haunt - ed with a mem - o - ry. _____ I

hate to say good - bye to the prai - rie. The

prai - rie is a part of me. _____

I Ride an Old Paint

Cowboy Song

draw, their tails are all mat - ted, their
fight, but still are he keeps sing - ing from
west, and we'll ride the prai - rie from that

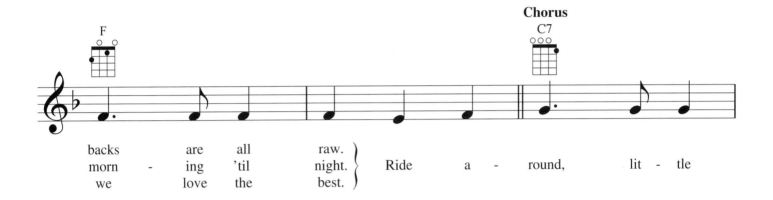

Chorus

backs are all raw. }
morn - ing 'til night. } Ride a - round, lit - tle
we love the best. }

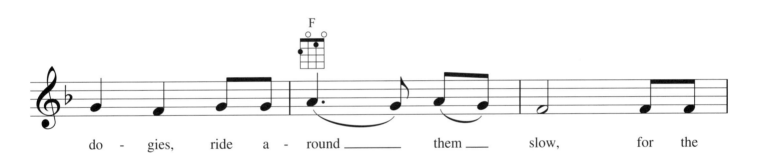

do - gies, ride a - round _____ them ___ slow, for the

1., 2.

fier - y and snuff - y are rar - in' to

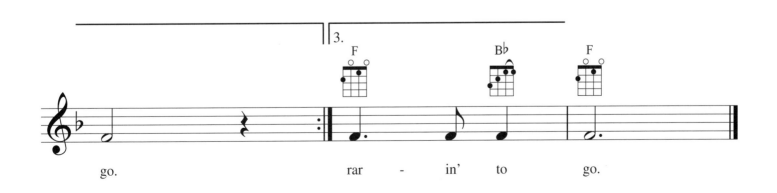

3.

go. rar - in' to go.

I Want to Be a Cowboy's Sweetheart

Words and Music by Patsy Montana

First note

Verse
Lively two-beat

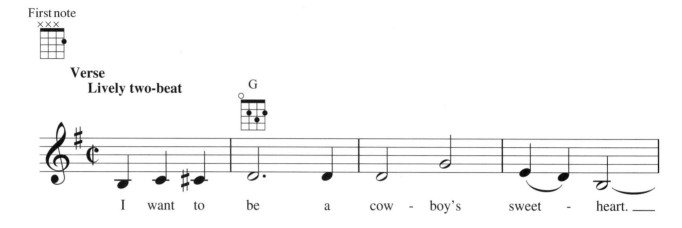

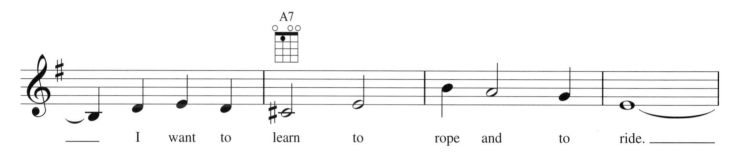

I want to be a cow-boy's sweet-heart. ____

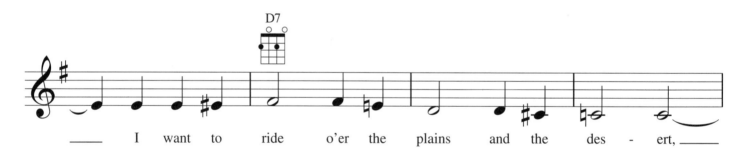

____ I want to learn to rope and to ride. ____

____ I want to ride o'er the plains and the des - ert, ____

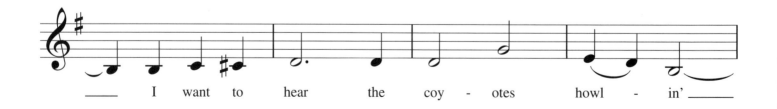

____ out west of the Great Di - vide. ____

____ I want to hear the coy - otes howl - in'

while the sun sets in the _____ west. _____

_____ I want to be a cow - boy's sweet -

heart; that's the life I love the best. _____

Chorus

_____ I want to ride old Paint, go - in' at a

run. I want to feel the wind in my face, _____

_____ a thou - sand miles _____ from the

49

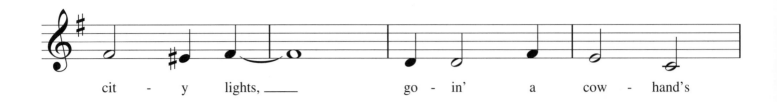

cit - y lights, _____ go - in' a cow - hand's

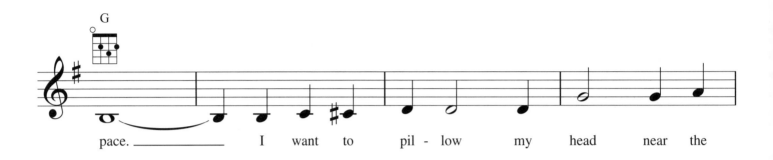

pace. _____ I want to pil - low my head near the

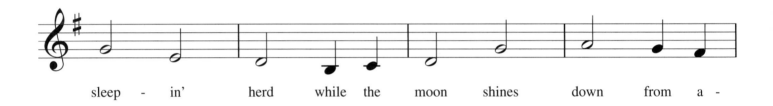

sleep - in' herd while the moon shines down from a -

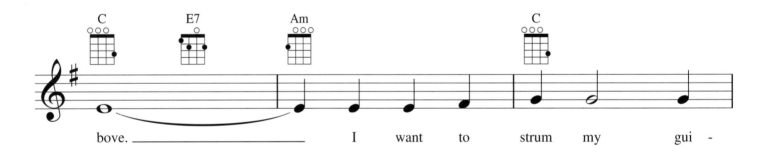

bove. _____ I want to strum my gui -

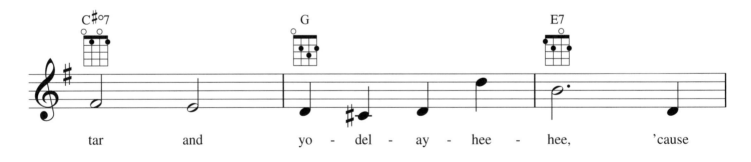

tar and yo - del - ay - hee - hee, 'cause

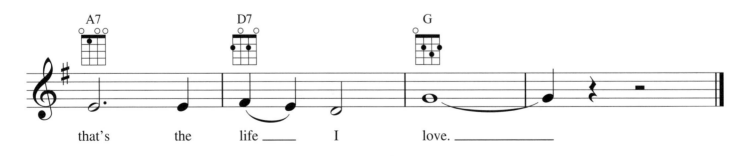

that's the life ___ I love. _____

The Last Roundup

Words and Music by Billy Hill

First note

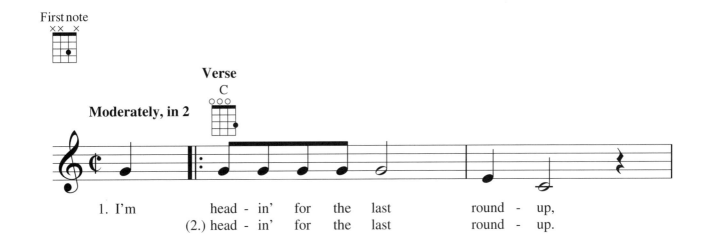

1. I'm   head - in'   for   the   last   round - up,
(2.) head - in'   for   the   last   round - up.

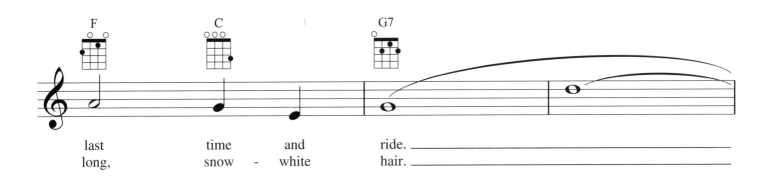

gon - na   sad - dle   Old   Paint   for   the
There'll be   Buf - fa - lo   Bill   with   his

last   time   and   ride. _____
long,   snow - white   hair. _____

_____   So   long,   old   pal,   it's
_____   There'll be   old   Kit   Car - son   and

time   your   tears   were   dried. _____
Cus - ter   wait - in'   there, _____

I'm   head - in'   for   the   last _____
a - rid - in'   in   the   last _____

Chorus

round - up.)
round - up.)
Git   a - long,   lit - tle   do - gie,   git   a -

long,   git   a - long.   Git   a - long,   lit - tle   do - gie,   git   a - long.   Git   a -

long,   lit - tle   do - gie,   git   a - long,   git   a - long.   Git   a - long,   lit - tle   do - gie,   git   a -

Outro-Verse

long.   I'm   head - in'   for   the   last   round - up,

to the   far - a - way   ranch   of   the   boss   in   the
gon - na   sad - dle   Old   Paint   for   the   last   time   and

sky. _____   Where   the
ride. _____   So _____

strays   are   count - ed   and   brand - ed,   there   go   I. _____
long,   old   pal, _____   it's   time   your   there   tears   were   dried. _____

_____   I'm

head - in'   for   the   last _____   round - up.

2. I'm   Git a - long,   lit - tle   do - gie,   git a - long.

I'm an Old Cowhand
(From the Rio Grande)
Words and Music by Johnny Mercer

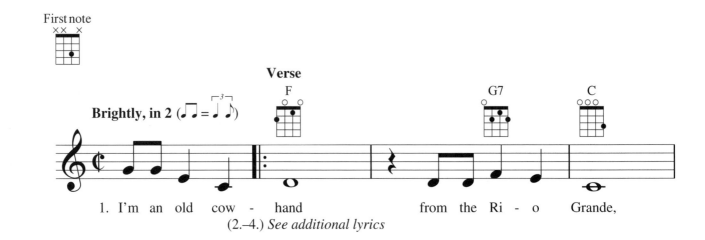

1. I'm an old cow - hand from the Ri - o Grande,
(2.–4.) *See additional lyrics*

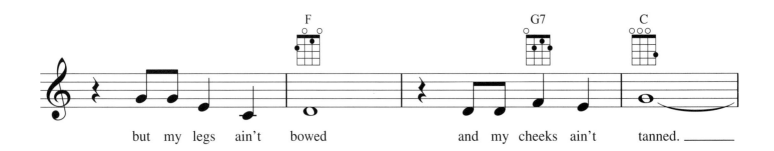

but my legs ain't bowed and my cheeks ain't tanned. _____

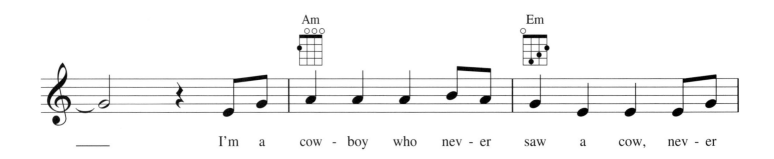

_____ I'm a cow - boy who nev - er saw a cow, nev - er

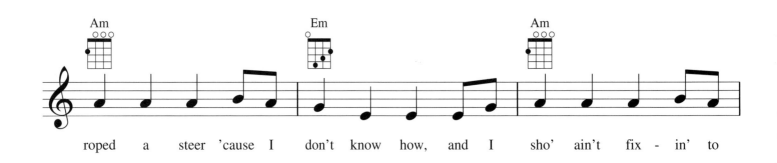

roped a steer 'cause I don't know how, and I sho' ain't fix - in' to

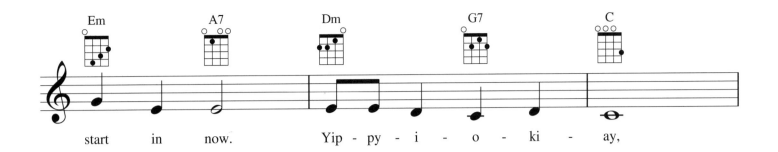

start   in   now.   Yip - py - i - o - ki - ay,

yip - py - i - o - ki - ay. 2.–4. I'm   an   old   cow - ay.

Additional Lyrics

2. I'm an old cowhand from the Rio Grande,
   And I learned to ride 'fore I learned to stand.
   I'm a ridin' fool who is up to date.
   I know ev'ry trail in the Lone Star State
   'Cause I ride the range in a Ford V8.
   Yippy-i-o-ki-ay, yippy-i-o-ki-ay.

3. I'm an old cowhand from the Rio Grande,
   And I come to town just to hear the band.
   I know all the songs that the cowboys know
   'Bout the big corral where the dogies go
   'Cause I learned them all on the radio.
   Yippy-i-o-ki-ay, yippy-i-o-ki-ay.

4. I'm an old cowhand from the Rio Grande,
   Where the West is wild 'round the Borderland,
   Where the buffalo roam around the zoo
   And the Indians make you a rug or two
   And the old Bar X is a Barbecue.
   Yippy-i-o-ki-ay, yippy-i-o-ki-ay.

Jesse James

Missouri Folksong

1. Jes - se James was a lad who ___ killed man - y a man. Once he
(2., 3.) *See additional lyrics*

robbed the Glen - dale ___ train. He would steal from the rich, he would

give to the poor, had a hand and a heart and a brain. Poor

Jes - se had a wife to ___ mourn for his life; three

chil - dren, they were brave. But the

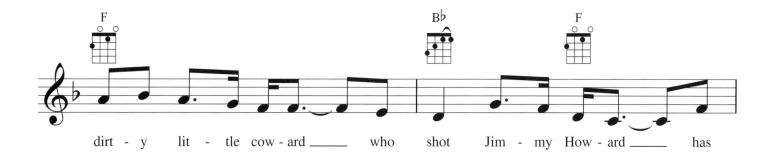

dirt - y   lit - tle   cow - ard _____   who   shot   Jim - my   How - ard _____   has

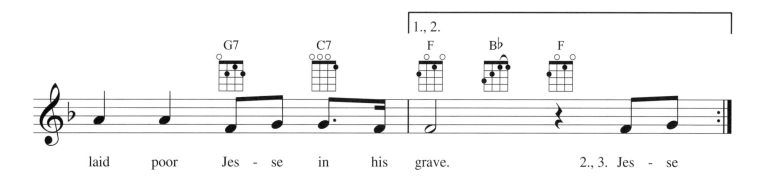

laid   poor   Jes - se   in   his   grave.   2., 3. Jes - se

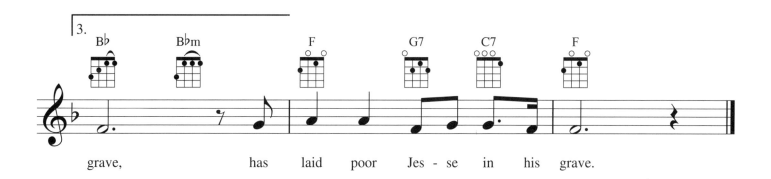

grave,   has   laid   poor   Jes - se   in   his   grave.

Additional Lyrics

2. Jesse James was a friend, and he helped ev'ryone out
   With a loot he stole from the bank.
   When a robb'ry occurred, no one had a doubt
   It was he and his dear brother Frank.
   Then one day Robert Ford, for the sake of reward,
   His word to the gov'nor gave.
   Oh, the dirty little coward who shot Jimmy Howard
   Has laid poor Jesse in his grave.

3. Jesse James took a name, "Jimmy Howard,"
   And flew to a town where he wasn't known.
   But his friend Robert Ford, neither faithful nor true,
   Turned against him and caught him alone.
   Poor Jesse, he was mourned, and his killer was scorned;
   How can friendship so behave?
   Oh, the dirty little coward who shot Jimmy Howard
   Has laid poor Jesse in his grave.

Jingle Jangle Jingle

(I Got Spurs)

from the Paramount Picture THE FOREST RANGERS

Words by Frank Loesser
Music by Joseph J. Lilley

Additional Lyrics

2. Oh, Mary Ann, oh, Mary Ann, Mary Ann,
   Though we done some moonlight walkin',
   This is why I up and ran:

3. Oh, Sally Jane, oh, Sally Jane, Sally Jane,
   Though I'd love to stay forever,
   This is why I can't remain:

4. Oh, Bessie Lou, oh, Bessie Lou, Bessie Lou,
   Though we done a heap of dreamin',
   This is why it won't come true:

Listen to the Rhythm of the Range

Words and Music by Gene Autry and Johnny Marvin

Mexicali Rose

from MEXICALI ROSE

Words by Helen Stone
Music by Jack B. Tenney

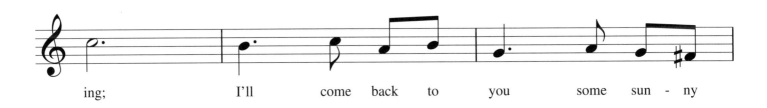

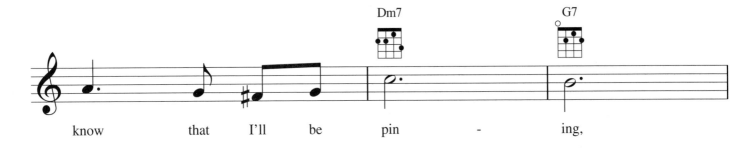

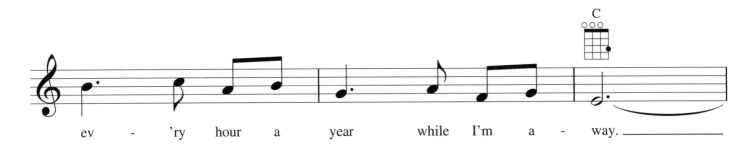

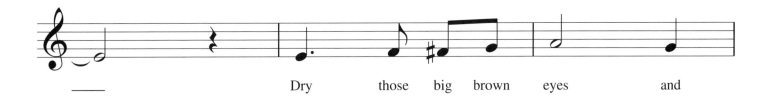

_____ Dry those big brown eyes and

smile, dear. Ban - ish all those

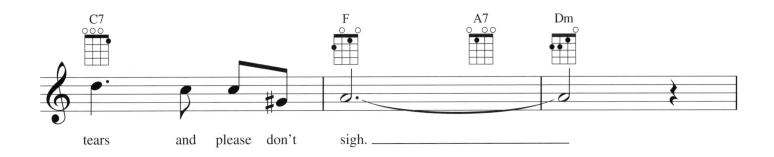

tears and please don't sigh. _____

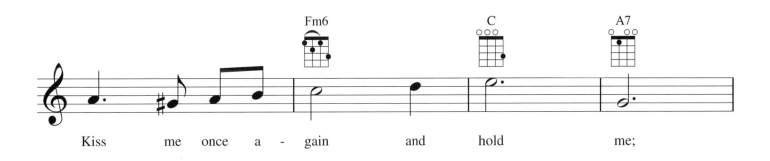

Kiss me once a - gain and hold me;

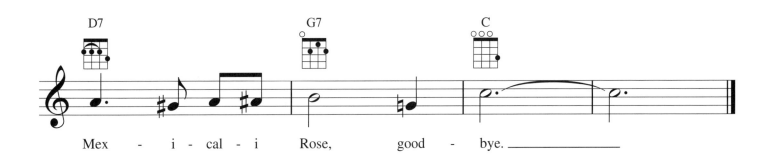

Mex - i - cal - i Rose, good - bye. _____

Mule Train

Words and Music by Johnny Lange, Hy Heath and Fred Glickman

First note

Chorus
Moderately bright, in 2

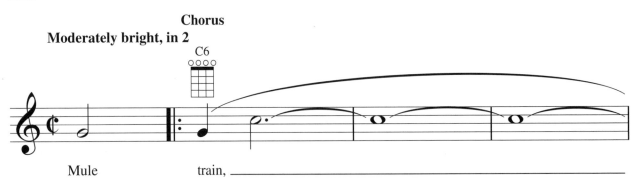

Mule   train, _____

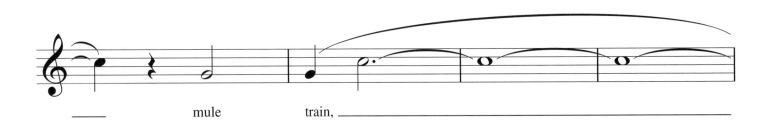

_____   mule   train, _____

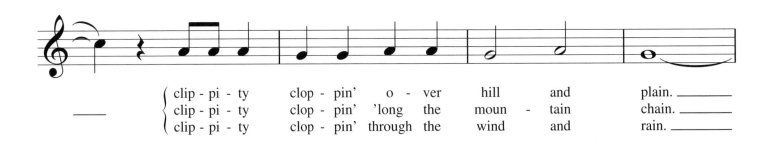

_____

clip - pi - ty   clop - pin'   o - ver   hill   and   plain. _____
clip - pi - ty   clop - pin'   'long   the   moun - tain   chain. _____
clip - pi - ty   clop - pin'   through   the   wind   and   rain. _____

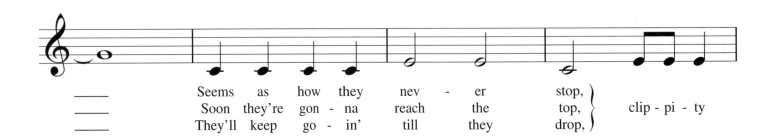

_____   Seems   as   how   they   nev - er   stop,⎫
_____   Soon   they're   gon - na   reach   the   top, ⎬   clip - pi - ty
_____   They'll   keep   go - in'   till   they   drop,⎭

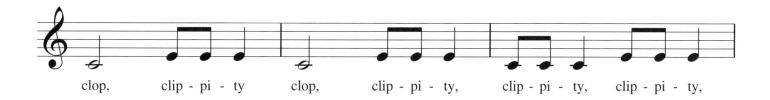

clop, clip - pi - ty clop, clip - pi - ty, clip - pi - ty, clip - pi - ty,

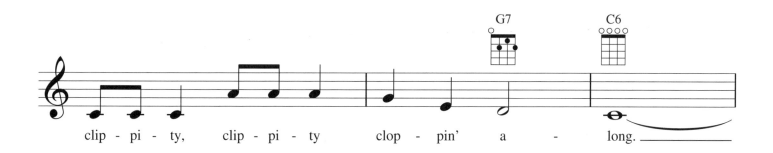

G7 C6

clip - pi - ty, clip - pi - ty clop - pin' a - long. _____

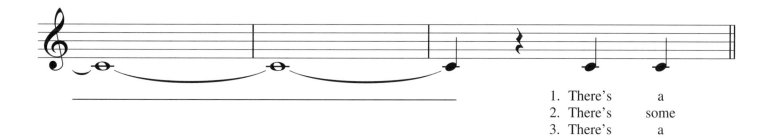

1. There's a
2. There's some
3. There's a

Verse

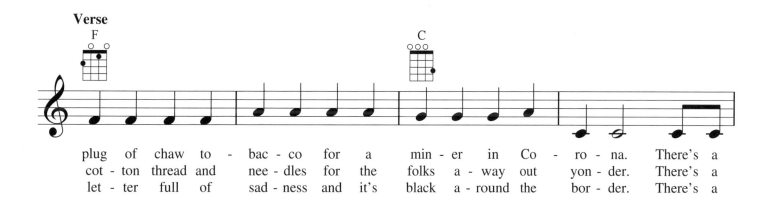

F   C

plug of chaw to - bac - co for a min - er in Co - ro - na. There's a
cot - ton thread and nee - dles for the folks a - way out yon - der. There's a
let - ter full of sad - ness and it's black a - round the bor - der. There's a

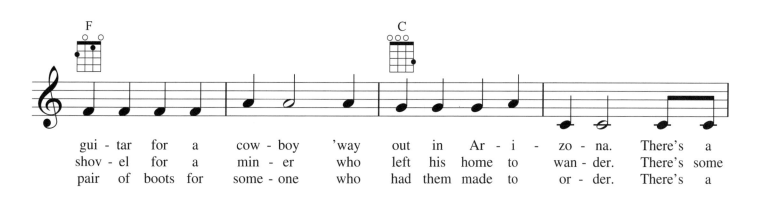

F   C

gui - tar for a cow - boy 'way out in Ar - i - zo - na. There's a
shov - el for a min - er who left his home to wan - der. There's some
pair of boots for some - one who had them made to or - der. There's a

dress of cal - i - co   for a   pret - ty Nav - a - jo.
rheu - ma - tis - m   pills   for the   set - tlers in the hills. } Git a -
Bi - ble in the pack   for the   Rev - 'rend Mis - ter Black.

long, _____   mule, _____   git a -

long. _____

1., 2.   3.   Outro

____ Mule ____   Git a - long, _____

____   mule, _____   git a -

long. _____

Little Joe, the Wrangler

Words and Music by N. Howard Thorp
Collected, Adapted and Arranged by John A. Lomax and Alan Lomax

First note

Verse
Brightly, in 2

1. It was Lit - tle Joe the wran - gler, he'll wran - gle nev - er -
(2.–5.) *See additional lyrics*

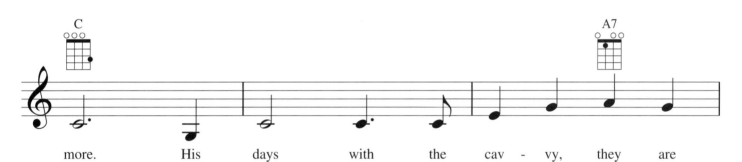

more. His days with the cav - vy, they are

done. _____ 'Twas a year a - go last

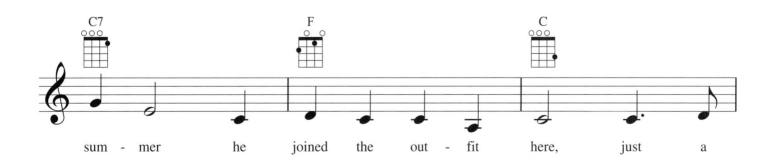

sum - mer he joined the out - fit here, just a

lit - tle Tex - as stray and all a - lone. _____

%. **Chorus**

_____ Well, it's long late in the eve - ning when he
(D.S.) morn - in' just at sun - up, _____ we

rode up to the herd on a lit - tle brown
found where Rock - et fell, down _____ in a wash - out

po - ny he called Chaw. _____ With his
for - ty feet be - low. _____ Be -

bro - ken shoes and o - ver - alls, a tough - er look - in'
neath his horse, mashed to a pulp, his spurs had rung the

To Coda ⊕

kid, well, I nev - er in my life had seen be -
knell for our lit - tle lost horse herd - er, wran - gler

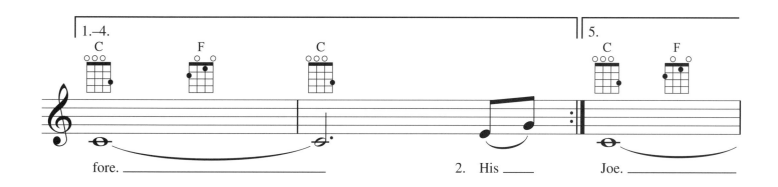

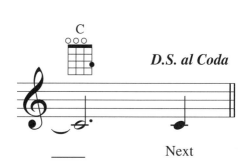

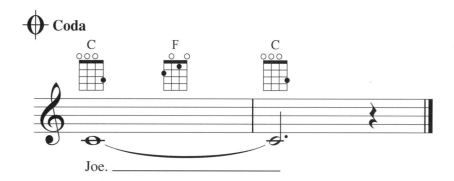

Additional Lyrics

2. His saddle was a southern kack
   Built many years ago,
   And an O.K. spur from one foot idly hung,
   While the hot roll in the cotton sack
   Was loosely tied behind,
   And a canteen from the saddle horn was slung.
   He said he'd had to leave his home,
   His ma had married twice,
   And his old man beat him ev'ry day or two.
   So he saddled up old Chaw one night
   And lit a chuck this way,
   Thought he'd try and paddle now his own canoe.

3. Said he'd try and do the best he could
   If we'd only give him work,
   But didn't know straight up about a cow.
   But the boss, he cuts him out a mount
   And kinder put him on,
   'Cause he sorta liked that little stray somehow.
   Taught him how to herd the horses
   And to know them all by name
   And to get them in by daylight if he could,
   And to follow the chuck wagon
   And to always hitch the team
   And to help the *cocinero rustle wood.

4. We was camped down in Red River
   And the weather, she was fine.
   We was settin' on the south side in a bend,
   When a Norther commenced blowin'
   And we all doubles up our guard,
   'Cause it took all hands to hold them cattle then.
   Well, little Joe the wrangler
   Was called out with the rest,
   And hardly had that kid got to the herd
   When them devils, they stampeded;
   Like a hailstorm 'long they flew,
   And all of us was ridin' for the lead.

5. 'Tween the streaks of lightnin' we could see
   That horse there out ahead.
   It was Little Joe the wrangler in the lead.
   He was ridin' old Blue Rocket with
   His slicker 'bove his head,
   A-tryin' to check them lead cows in their speed.
   Well, we got them kinda millin'
   And sorta quieted down,
   And the extra guard back to the camp did go.
   But one of them was missin',
   And we all saw at a glance
   'Twas our little lost horse herder, wrangler Joe.

* Spanish word for a cook.

My Old Saddle Pal

Words and Music by Gene Autry and Odie Thompson

First note

Verse
Moderate Waltz

1. When the round-up time is o-ver _____
2. But they're leav-in' one be-hind them, _____

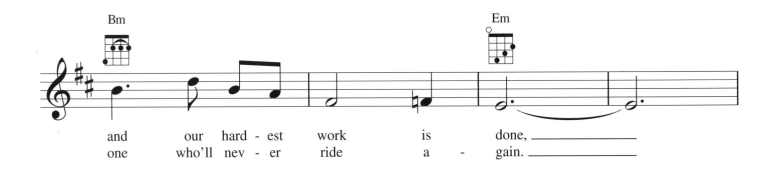

and our hard-est work is done, _____
one who'll nev-er ride a-gain. _____

cow-boys sad-dlin' up their po-nies, _____
All the cow-boys' hearts are heav-y. _____

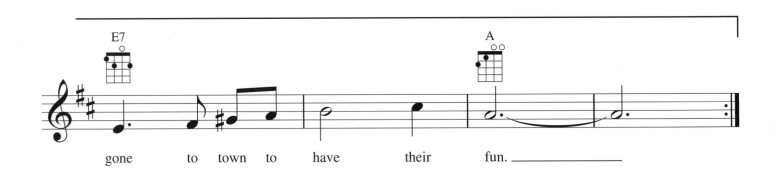

gone to town to have their fun. _____

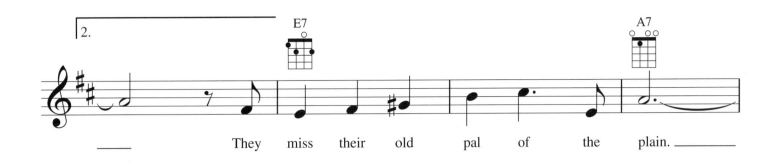

2.

E7　　　　　　　　　　　　　　　　　　　　　A7

_____ They miss their old pal of the plain. _____

Chorus

D　　　　　　　　　A7　　　　　　　　D

_____ How I miss the voice of my old sad - dle

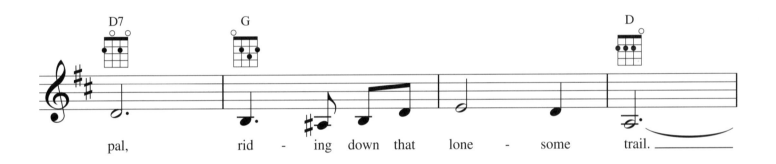

D7　　　　G　　　　　　　　　　　　　　　D

pal, rid - ing down that lone - some trail. _____

A7　　　　　　　　　D

_____ I miss him when I'm sit - ting by the side of my

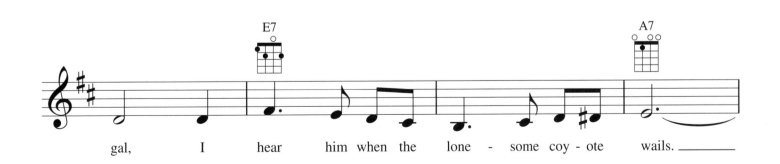

E7　　　　　　　　　　　　　　　A7

gal, I hear him when the lone - some coy - ote wails. _____

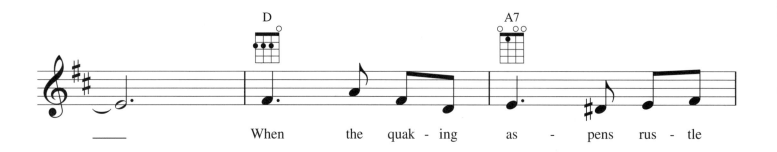

When   the quak - ing   as - pens rus - tle

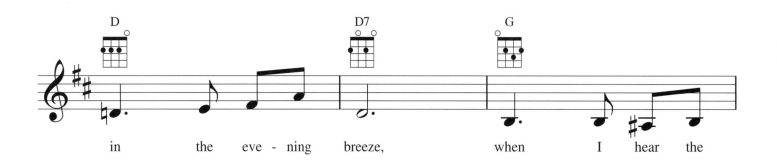

in   the eve - ning breeze,   when   I   hear the

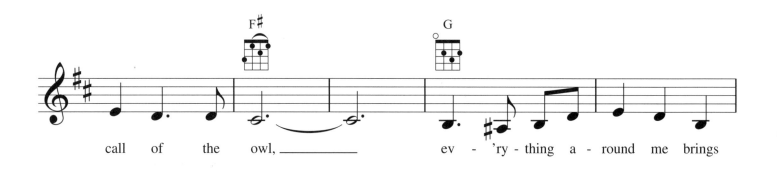

call   of   the owl, _____   ev - 'ry - thing a - round me brings

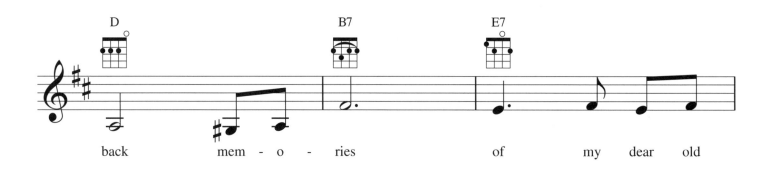

back   mem - o - ries   of   my   dear old

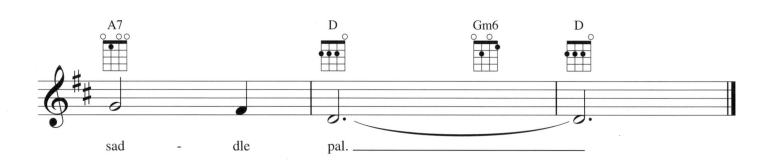

sad - dle   pal. _____

The Red River Valley

Traditional American Cowboy Song

Pecos Bill

from Walt Disney's MELODY TIME

Words by Johnny Lange
Music by Eliot Daniel

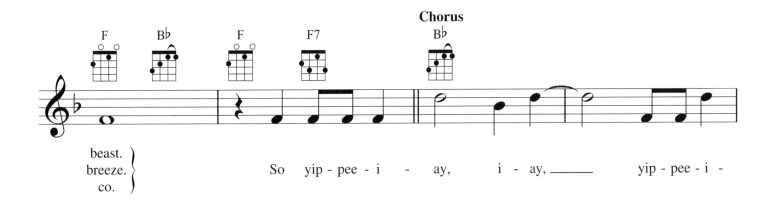

beast.
breeze.
co.

So yip - pee - i - ay, i - ay, _____ yip - pee - i -

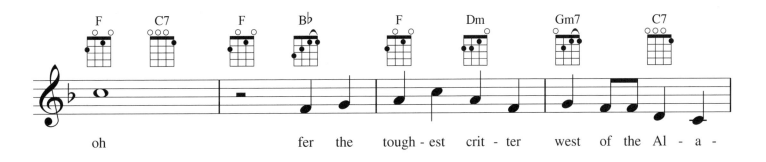

oh fer the tough - est crit - ter west of the Al - a -

1.–6. mo.   2. Once he   **7.** mo. _____
                            3. Once there
                            4. Once a

Additional Lyrics

4. Once a band of rustlers stole a herd of cattle,
   But they didn't know the herd they stole was Bill's.
   And when he caught them crooked vill'ins,
   Pecos knocked out all their fillins;
   That's the reason why there's gold in them thar hills.

5. Pecos lost his way while trav'lin' on the desert.
   It was ninety miles across the burnin' sand.
   He knew he'd never reach the border
   If he didn't get some water,
   So he got a stick and dug the Rio Grande.

6. While a tribe of painted Injuns did a war dance,
   Pecos started shootin' up their little game.
   He gave them redskins such a shakeup
   That they jumped out from their makeup;
   That's the way the Painted Desert got its name.

7. While reclinin' on a cloud high over Texas,
   With his gun he made the stars evaporate.
   Then Pecos saw the stars declinin',
   So he left one brightly shinin'
   As the emblem of the Lone Star Texas State.

Pistol Packin' Mama

Words and Music by Al Dexter

First note

Verse
Bright Country, in 2

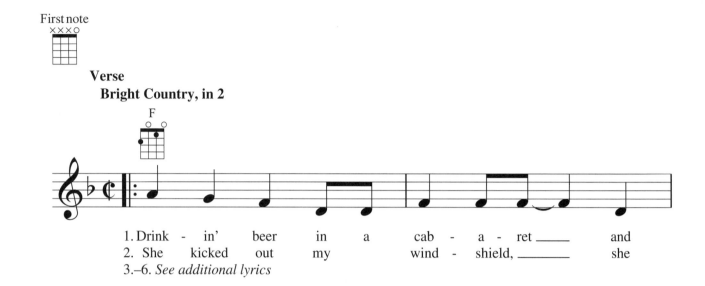

1. Drink - in' beer in a cab - a - ret _____ and
2. She kicked out my wind - shield, _____ she
3.–6. *See additional lyrics*

was I hav - in' fun! Un - til one night she
hit me o - ver the head. She cussed and cried and

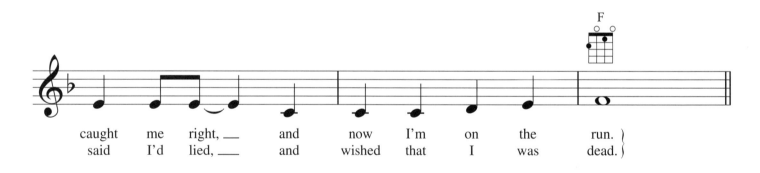

caught me right, ___ and now I'm on the run. }
said I'd lied, ___ and now wished that I was dead. }

Chorus

Lay that pis - tol down, babe, lay that pis - tol

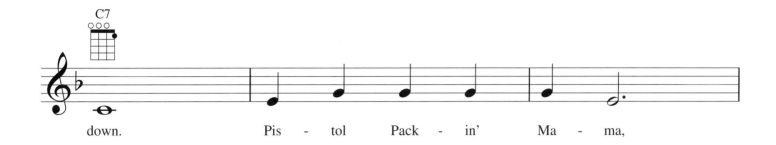

down.   Pis - tol   Pack - in'   Ma - ma,

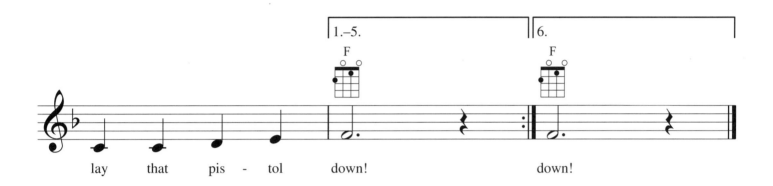

lay   that   pis - tol   down!   down!

Additional Lyrics

3. Drinkin' beer in a cabaret
   And dancing with a blonde,
   Until one night she shot out the light.
   Bang! That blonde was gone.

4. I'll see you ev'ry night, babe,
   I'll woo you ev'ry day.
   I'll be your regular daddy
   If you'll put that gun away.

5. Drinkin' beer in a cabaret
   And was havin' fun,
   Until one night she caught me right,
   And now I'm on the run.

6. Now there was old Al Dexter,
   He always had his fun.
   But with some lead, she shot him dead.
   His honkin' days were done.

The Rambling Gambler

Collected, Adapted and Arranged by John A. Lomax and Alan Lomax

First note

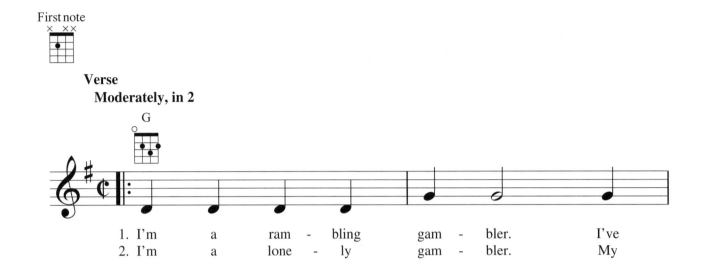

Verse
Moderately, in 2

1. I'm a ram - bling gam - bler. I've
2. I'm a lone - ly gam - bler. My

gam - bled all a - round. Wher -
dreams don't win a thing. When -

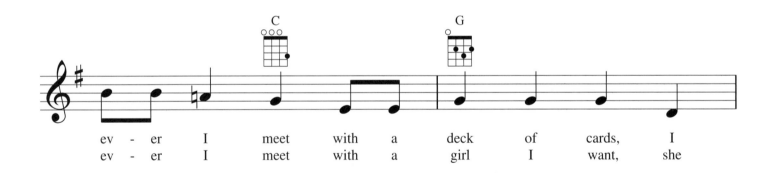

ev - er I meet with a deck of cards, I
ev - er I meet with a girl I want, she

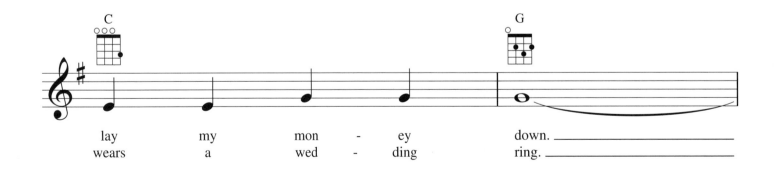

lay my mon - ey down. _____
wears a wed - ding ring. _____

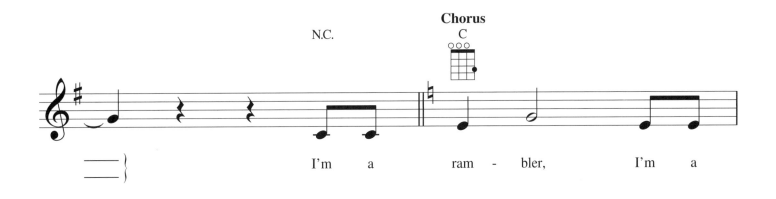

N.C.

Chorus

C

I'm a ram - bler, I'm a

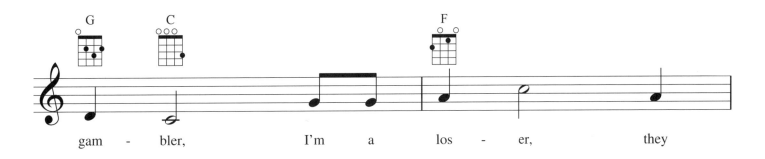

G C F

gam - bler, I'm a los - er, they

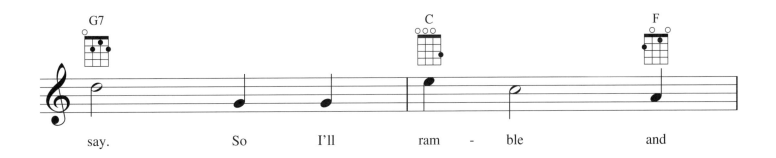

G7 C F

say. So I'll ram - ble and

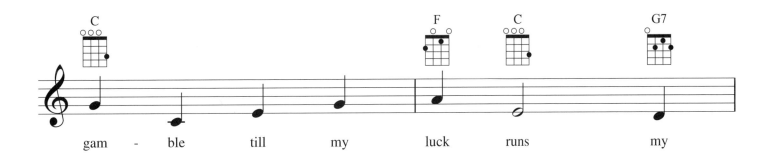

C F C G7

gam - ble till my luck runs my

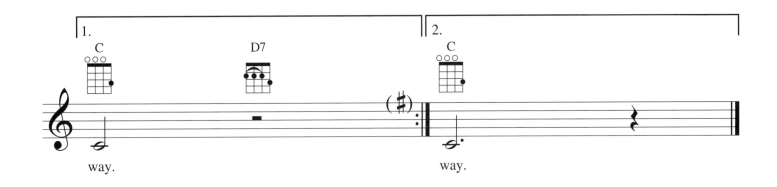

1. C D7 2. C

way. way.

Sing Me a Song of the Saddle

Words and Music by Gene Autry and Frank Harford

First note

Verse
Moderately

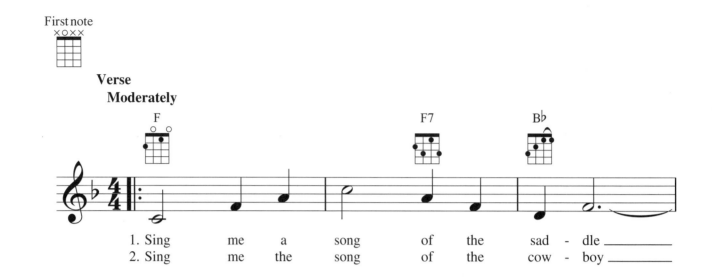

1. Sing me a song of the sad - dle _____
2. Sing me the song of the cow - boy _____

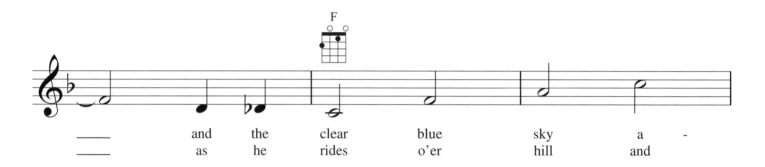

_____ and the clear blue sky a -
_____ as he rides o'er hill and

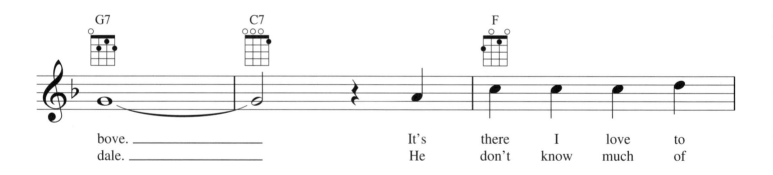

bove. _____ It's there I love to
dale. _____ He don't know much of

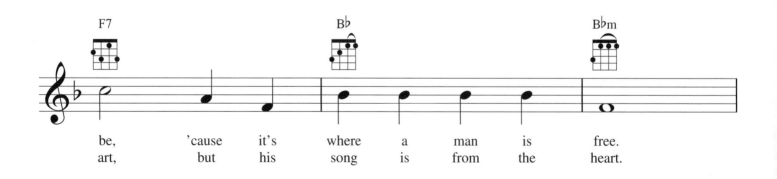

be, 'cause it's where a man is free.
art, but his song is from the heart.

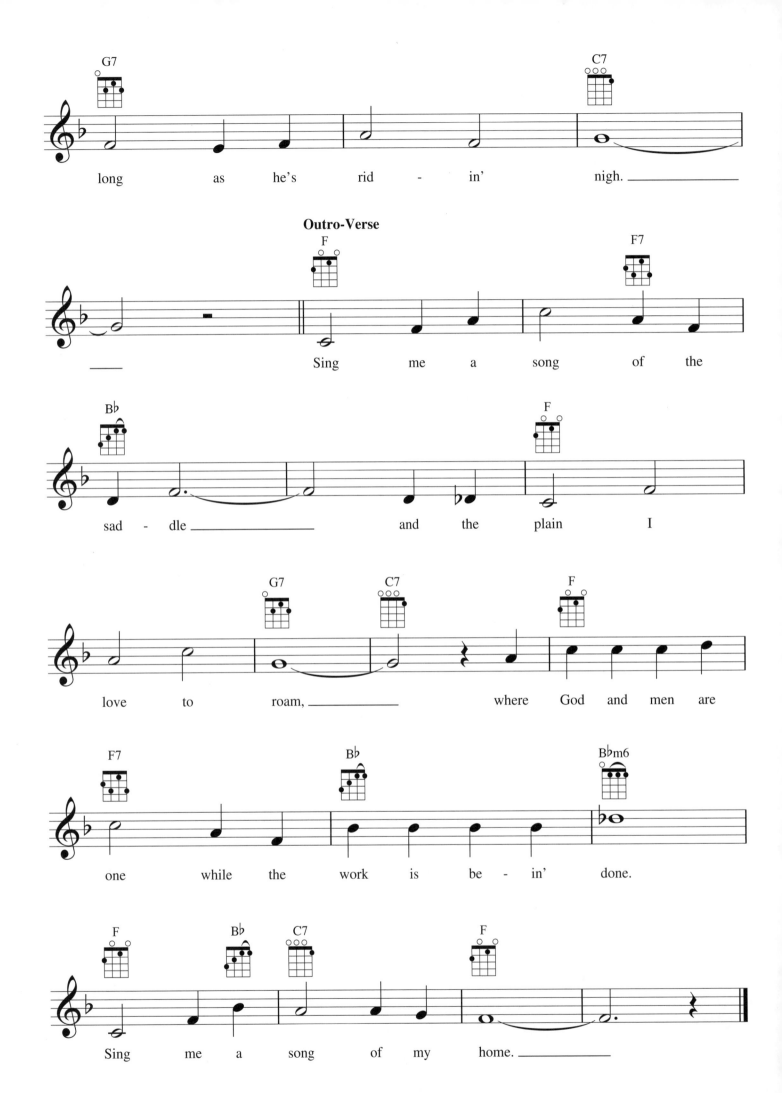

Outro-Verse

82

Take Me Back to My Boots and Saddle

Words and Music by Walter Samuels, Teddy Powell and Leonard Whitcup

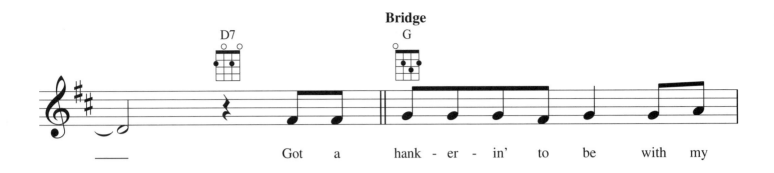

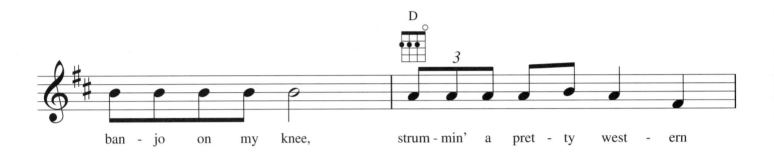

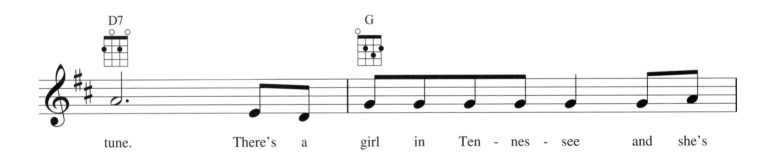

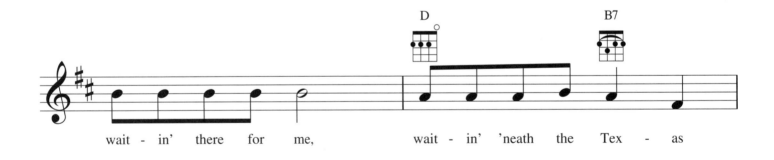

Sioux City Sue

Words by Ray Freedman
Music by Dick Thomas

First note

Verse
Moderately, in 2

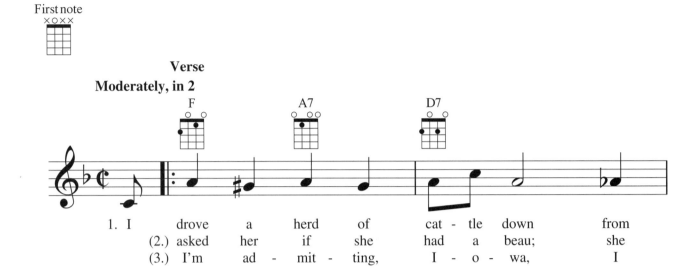

1. I drove a herd of cat - tle down from
(2.) asked her if she had a beau; she
(3.) I'm ad - mit - ting, I - o - wa, I

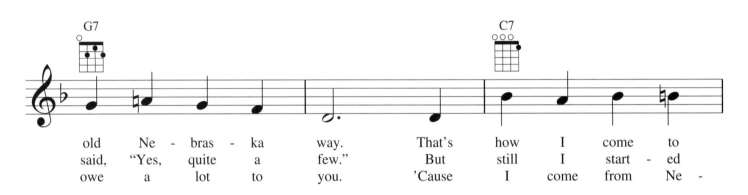

old Ne - bras - ka way. That's how I come to
said, "Yes, quite a few." But still I come start - ed
owe a lot to you. 'Cause I come from Ne -

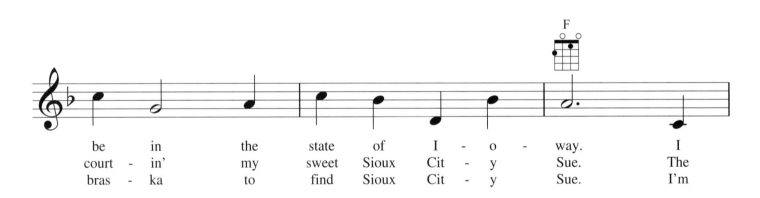

be in the state of I - o - way. I
court - in' my sweet Sioux Cit - y Sue. The
bras - ka to find Sioux Cit - y Sue. I'm

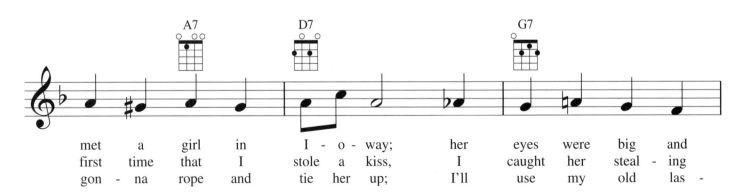

met a girl in I - o - way; her eyes were big and
first time that I stole a kiss, I caught her steal - ing
gon - na rope and tie her up; I'll use my old las -

blue.   I asked her what her name was; she
two.   I asked her what did she love me; she
so.   I'm gon - na put my brand on my

Chorus

said, "Sioux Cit - y Sue."   Sioux Cit - y Sue, _____
said, "In - deed I do." }
sweet Sioux Cit - y Sue. }

Sioux Cit - y Sue, _____ your hair is red, your eyes are blue. I'd

swap my horse and dog for you. ___ Sioux Cit - y Sue, _____

Sioux Cit - y Sue. _____ There ain't no gal as true as my

1., 2.

3.

sweet Sioux Cit - y Sue.   2. I   Sue.
3. Now,

Streets of Laredo
(The Cowboy's Lament)
Collected, Adapted and Arranged by John A. Lomax and Alan Lomax

First note

Verse

With a lilt

1. As I _____ walked out in the streets of La -
(2.–7.) See additional lyrics

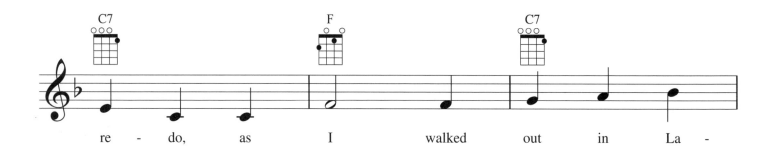

re - do, as I walked out in La -

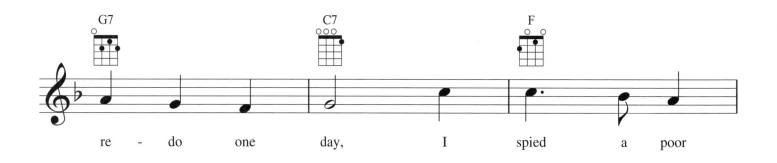

re - do one day, I spied a poor

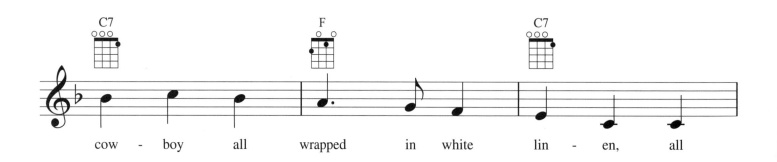

cow - boy all wrapped in white lin - en, all

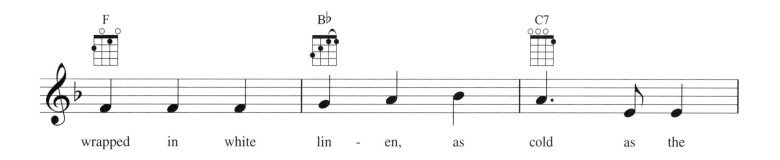

wrapped   in   white   lin - en,   as   cold   as   the

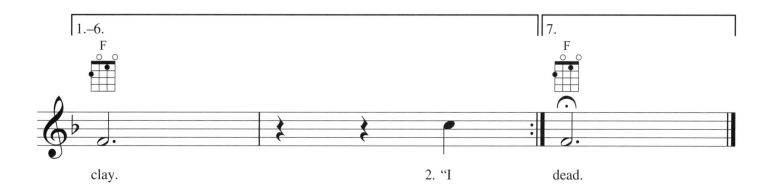

clay.   2. "I   dead.

Additional Lyrics

2. "I see by your outfit that you are a cowboy."
   These words he did say as I calmly went by.
   "Come sit down beside me and hear my sad story.
   I'm shot in the breast and I know I must die."

3. "It was once in the saddle I used to go dashing,
   With no one as quick on the trigger as I.
   I sat in a card game in back of the barroom.
   Got shot in the back and today I must die."

4. "Get six of my buddies to carry my coffin,
   And six pretty maidens to sing a sad song.
   Take me to the valley and lay the sod o'er me,
   For I'm a young cowboy who played the game wrong."

5. "Oh, beat the drum slowly and play the fife lowly,
   And play the dead march as they carry my pall.
   Put bunches of roses all over my coffin;
   The roses will deaden the clods as they fall."

6. "Go gather around you a crowd of young cowboys,
   And tell them the story of this my sad fate.
   Tell one and the other before they go further,
   To stop their wild roving before it's too late."

7. "Go fetch me a cup, just a cup of cold water
   To cool my parched lips," the cowboy then said.
   Before I returned, his brave spirit had left him,
   And, gone to his Maker, the cowboy was dead.

South of the Border

(Down Mexico Way)

Words and Music by Jimmy Kennedy and Michael Carr

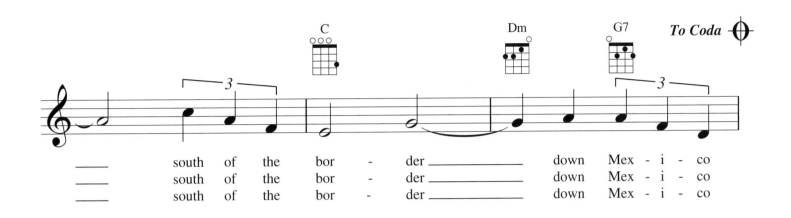

south of the bor - der _____ down Mex - i - co
south of the bor - der _____ down Mex - i - co
south of the bor - der _____ down Mex - i - co

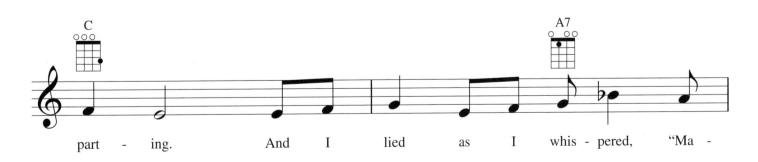

way. _____ 2. She was a way. _____

Bridge

___ Then she sighed as she whis - pered, "Ma -

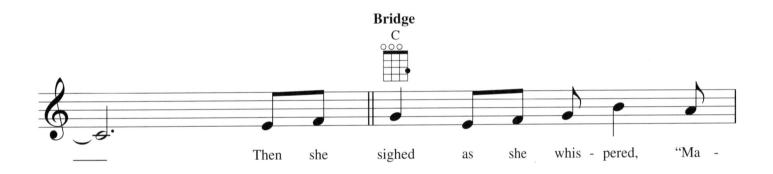

ña - na," nev - er dream - ing that we were

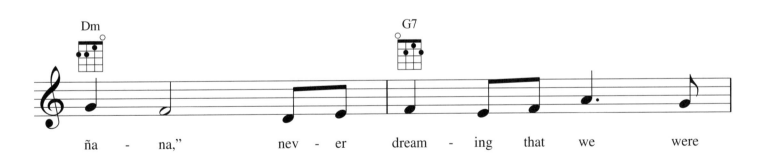

part - ing. And I lied as I whis - pered, "Ma -

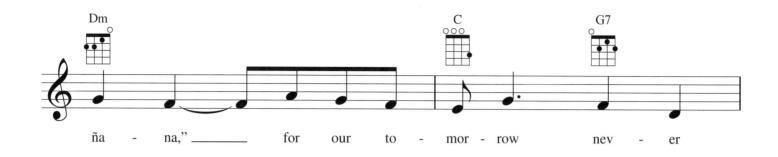

ña - na," _____ for our to - mor - row nev - er

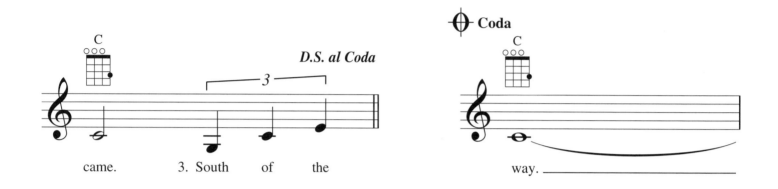

came. 3. South of the

D.S. al Coda

⊕ **Coda**

way. _____

Outro

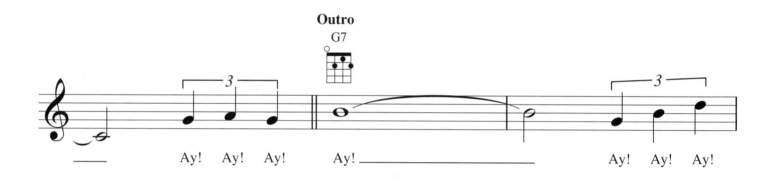

___ Ay! Ay! Ay! Ay! _____ Ay! Ay! Ay!

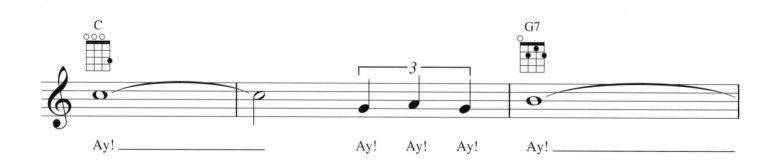

Ay! _____ Ay! Ay! Ay! Ay! _____

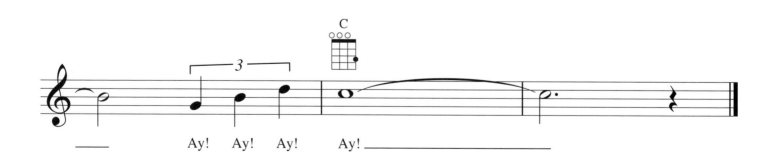

___ Ay! Ay! Ay! Ay! _____

That Silver Haired Daddy of Mine

Words and Music by Gene Autry and Jimmy Long

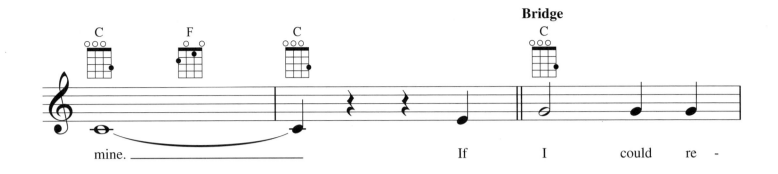

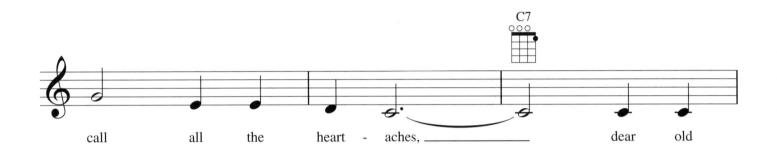

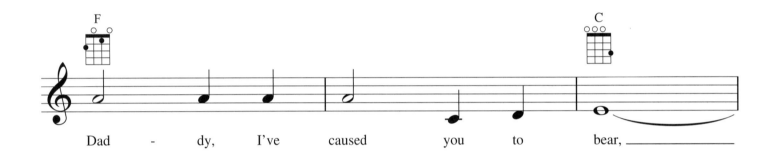

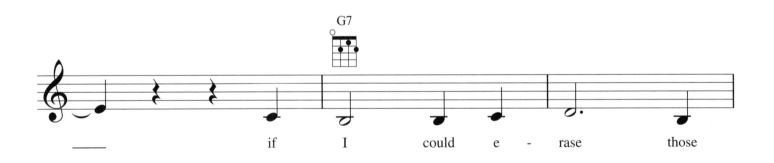

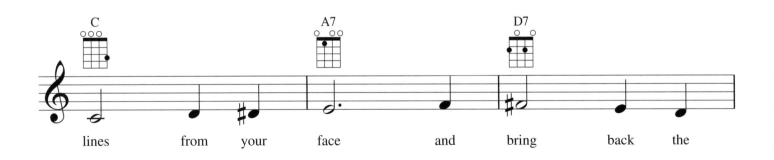

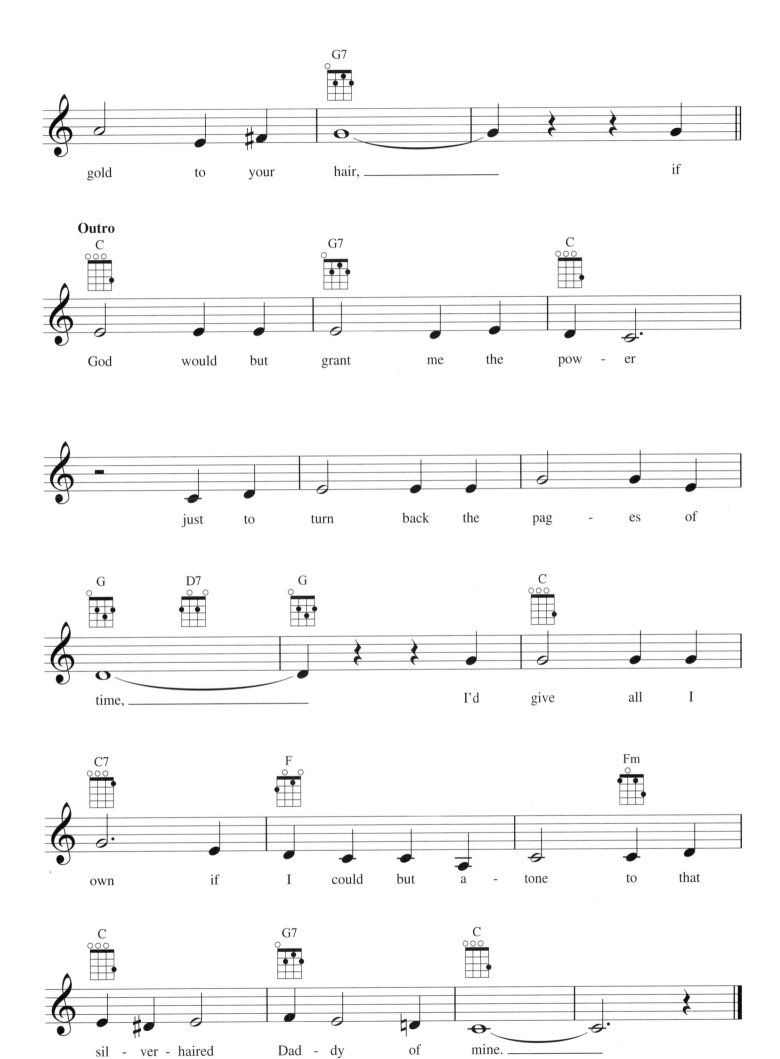

gold   to   your   hair, _____   if

Outro

God   would   but   grant   me   the   pow - er

just   to   turn   back   the   pag - es   of

time, _____   I'd   give   all   I

own   if   I   could   but   a - tone   to   that

sil - ver - haired   Dad - dy   of   mine. _____

Teardrops in My Heart

Words and Music by Vaughn Horton

First note

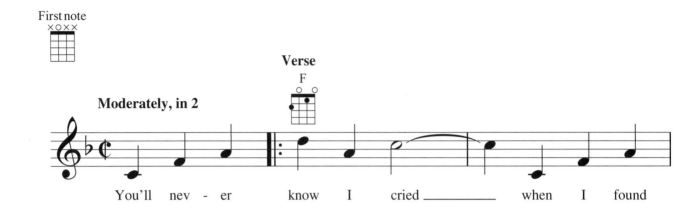

Moderately, in 2

You'll nev - er know I cried _____ when I found

out you lied, _____ for I've been hid - in' all the

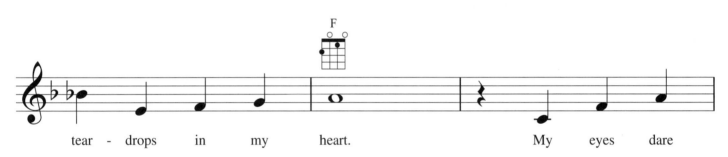

tear - drops in my heart. My eyes dare

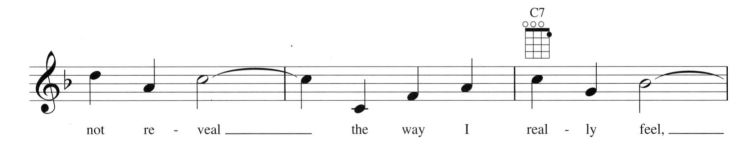

not re - veal _____ the way I real - ly feel, _____

_____ be - cause I know I'll pour my heart out if I

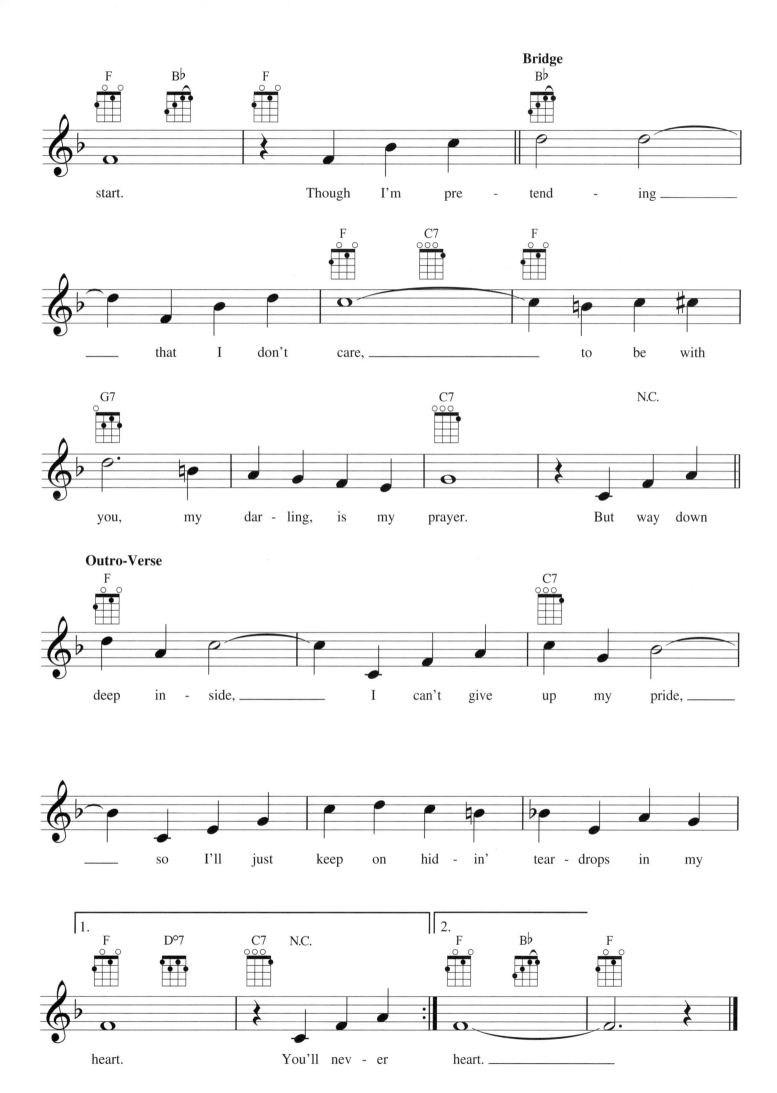

start.   Though   I'm   pre - tend - ing _____

_____ that   I   don't   care, _____ to   be   with

you,   my   dar - ling,   is   my   prayer.   But   way   down

deep   in - side, _____   I   can't   give   up   my   pride, _____

_____ so   I'll   just   keep   on   hid - in'   tear - drops   in   my

heart.   You'll nev - er   heart. _____

There's an Empty Cot in the Bunkhouse Tonight

Words and Music by Gene Autry and Smiley Burnette

where the fore-man takes care of his own. _____ There'll

be an emp-ty sad-dle to-night, but he's hap-py up

1.–3.
there, _____ I know. 2. He was

4.
bove. _____

Additional Lyrics

2. He was riding the range last Saturday noon
   When a Norther had started to blow.
   His head in his chest, heading into the west,
   He was stopped by a cry soft and low.
   There a crazy young calf had strayed from his ma
   And was lost in the snow and the storm.
   He lay in a heap at the end of the draw,
   Huddled all in a bunch to keep warm.

3. Limpy hobbled his feet, tossed him over his hoss
   And started again for the shack.
   But the wind got cold and the snow piled up,
   And poor Limpy strayed from his track.
   He arrived at three in the morning
   And put the maverick to bed,
   And flopped in his bunk not able to move;
   This morning old Limpy was dead.

4. There's a cot unused in the bunkhouse tonight,
   There's a Pinto's head hanging low.
   The spurs and caps hang on the wall;
   Limpy's gone where the good cowboys go.
   There's a place for every cowboy
   Who has that kind of love,
   And someday he'll ride old Pinto
   On that range up there above.

Twilight on the Trail

Words by Sidney Mitchell
Music by Sidney Mitchell and Louis Alter

2. When it's

Freely
Bridge

Nev - er ev - er have a nick - el in my jeans. Nev - er ev - er have a debt to

pay. Still, I un - der - stand what real con - tent - ment means;

Tempo I

D.S. al Coda

guess I was born that way. _____ 3. When it's

Coda

Outro

Slower

When it's twi - light

on the trail. _____

Wagon Wheels

Words by Billy Hill
Music by Peter DeRose

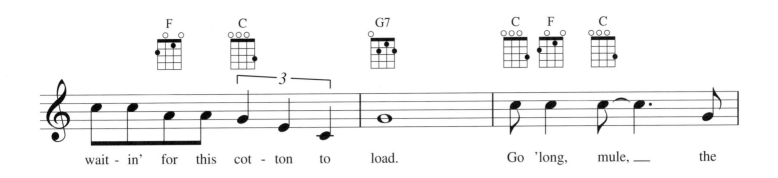

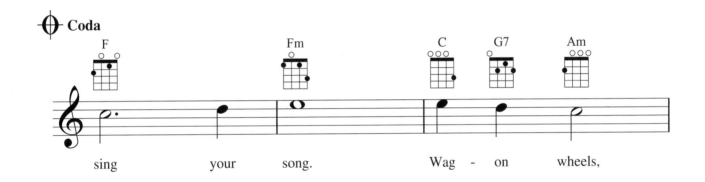
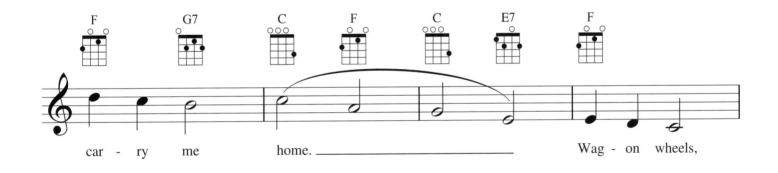
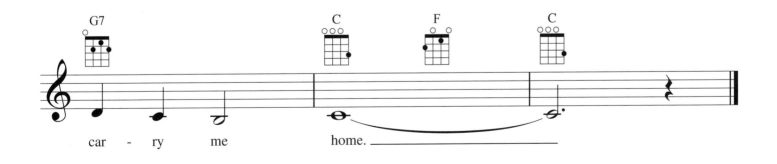

The Wild Rippling Water

Collected, Adapted and Arranged by John A. Lomax and Alan Lomax

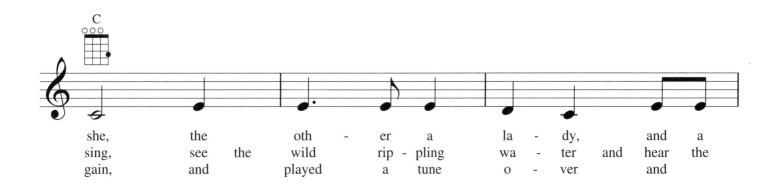

she,   the   oth - er   a   la - dy,   and   a

sing,   see the   wild   rip - pling   wa - ter and hear the

gain,   and   played   a tune   o - ver   and

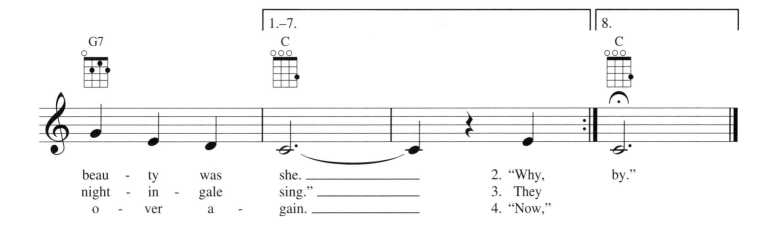

beau - ty   was   she. _____   2. "Why,   by."

night - in - gale   sing." _____   3. They

o - ver   a - gain. _____   4. "Now,"

Additional Lyrics

4. "Now," says the cowboy, "I should have been gone."
"No, no," said the maid, "just play one more song.
I'd rather hear the fiddle played on one string
Than to see the wild water and hear the nightingale sing,
See the wild rippling water and hear the nightingale sing."

5. He tuned up his fiddle and rosined his bow
And played her a lecture, he played it all low.
He played her a lecture all on the high string.
"Hark, hark," said the maid, "hear the nightingale sing."
"Hark, hark," said the maid, "hear the nightingale sing."

6. She says, "Dear cowboy, will you marry me?"
"No, no, pretty maid, that never can be.
I've a wife in Arizona, a lady is she.
One wife and one ranch are plenty for me,
One wife and one ranch are plenty for me."

7. "I'll go to Mexico and I'll stay there one year,
I'll drink a lot of wine, I'll drink a lot of beer.
If I even come back, it will be in the spring
To see the wild water and hear the nightingale sing,
See the wild rippling water and hear the nightingale sing."

8. Come, all you young ladies, take warning from me:
Never place your affections in a cowboy so free.
He'll go away and leave you as mine left me,
Leave you rocking the cradle, singing "Bye, oh, baby,"
Leave you rocking the cradle, singing "Bye, oh, baby."

The Yellow Rose of Texas

Words and Music by J.K., 1858

Chorus

nev - er - more will part.
not to leave her so.
mine for - ev - er - more.

She's the sweet - est rose of col - or this fel - low ev - er knew. Her eyes are bright as dia - monds, they spar - kle like the dew. You may talk a - bout your dear - est May, and sing of Ro - sa Lee. But the Yel - low Rose of Tex - as beats the belles of Ten - nes - see.

When It's Night Time in Nevada

Words and Music by Richard Pascoe, Will Dulmage and H.O. Reilly Clint

First note

Gentle Waltz

When it's night time in Ne - va - da, I'm ___

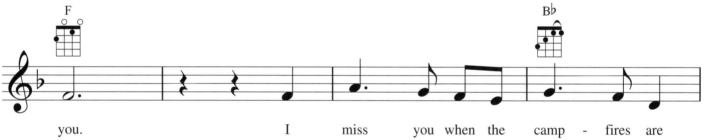

dream - in' ___ of the old days on the des - ert and

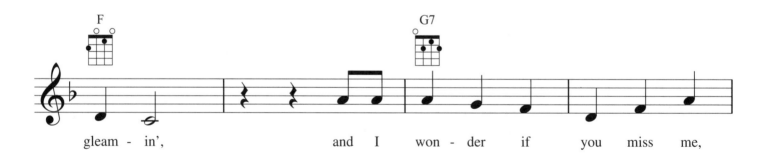

you. I miss you when the camp - fires are

gleam - in', and I won - der if you miss me,

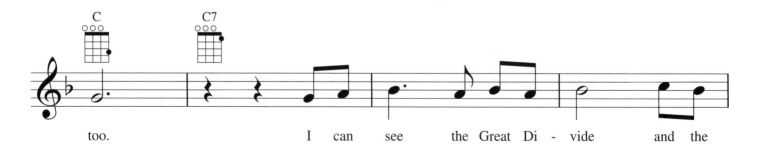

too. I can see the Great Di - vide and the

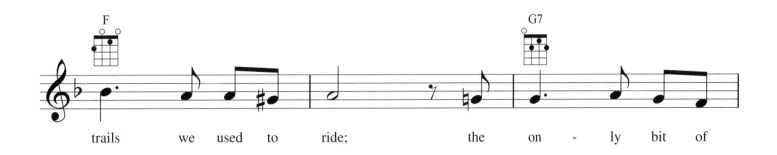

trails   we   used   to   ride;   the   on -   ly   bit   of

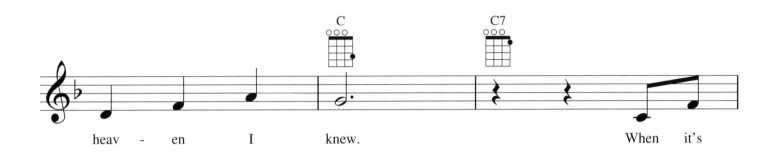

heav -   en   I   knew.   When   it's

night   time   in   Ne -   va -   da,   I'm ____ dream - in' _____

To Coda ⊕

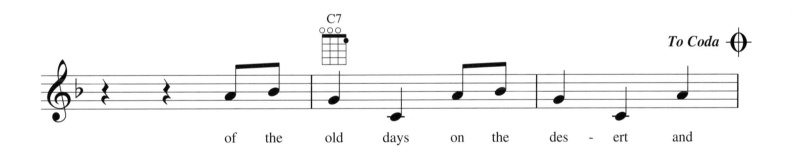

of   the   old   days   on   the   des -   ert   and

Bridge

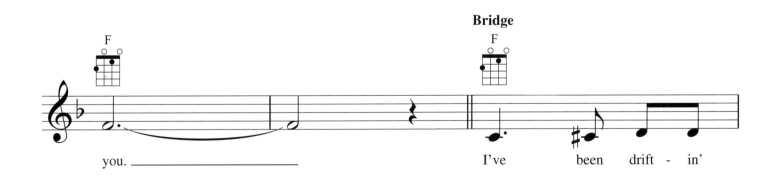

you. _____   I've   been   drift - in'

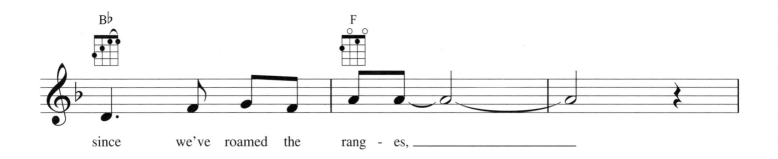

since   we've roamed the   rang - es, _____

up   to roam - in'   when   you   went   a -   way, _____

_____   with   the love for   you   that nev - er chang - es. ____

I   hope   that   we   will   meet   a - gain some -

D.S. al Coda

⊕ Coda

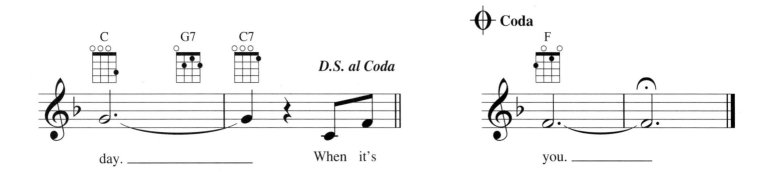

day. _____   When it's   you. _____